The L. Ron Hubbard Series

BRIDGE PUBLICATIONS, INC.
5600 E. Olympic Blvd.
Commerce, California 90022 USA

ISBN 978-1-4031-9891-4

Special acknowledgment is made to the L. Ron Hubbard Library for permission to reproduce photographs from his personal collection. Additional credits: pp. 1, 9, 27, 61, 75, back cover Dman/Shutterstock.com; pp. 2–3 Luril Konoval/Shutterstock. com; pp. 19, 23, 53, 55 kanate/Shutterstock.com; pp. 58–59 silver-john/Shutterstock.com; p. 60 Anton Petrus/Shutterstock.com.

Printed in the United States of America

The L. Ron Hubbard Series: Rehabilitating a Drugged Society—English

The *Purification* and Narconon New Life Detoxification programs cannot be construed as a recommendation of medical treatment or medication and it is not professed as a physical handling for bodies nor is any claim made to that effect. There are no medical recommendations or claims for the *Purification* or Narconon New Life Detoxification programs or for any of the vitamin or mineral regimens described in this publication.

No individual should undertake the *Purification* or Narconon New Life Detoxification programs or any of its regimens without first consulting and obtaining the informed approval of a licensed medical practitioner. Neither the author nor the publisher make any warranties or representations as to the effectiveness of the *Purification* and Narconon New Life Detoxification programs.

The L. Ron Hubbard Series

HUMANITARIAN
REHABILITATING
A DRUGGED
SOCIETY

Bridge

PUBLICATIONS, INC.®

CONTENTS

An Introduction to
L. Ron Hubbard

WE SHALL EXAMINE WHAT LRH DISCOVERIES HAVE revealed regarding drugs as an agent of societal control and "other brutal truths" of this subject. The drug prevention and rehabilitation methods of L. Ron Hubbard are presently employed in some fifty nations and credited with the salvation

of at least a million at-risk people. Included therein are tens of thousands of otherwise terminal addicts and many recreational users. His discoveries relating to the biochemical action of drugs and toxins are universally acclaimed as landmark, while with an unparalleled success rate among previously incurable amphetamine, cocaine and opiate users, the word is *benchmark*—as in, here is the rehabilitation program against which all other programs are measured.

How L. Ron Hubbard came to discover the world's most effective solution to drug addiction and what that discovery represents to a culture in the grip of a monumental drug-abuse crisis is the subject of this publication. Those who know the initials LRH only for his founding of Dianetics and

Scientology will find this story altogether enlightening; for here is both another dimension to the man and what a spiritual technology can accomplish in the face of physical craving. Those active in the fields of drug enforcement, prevention and treatment will likewise find this publication a revelation; for here, in all truth, is what you have been searching for or what you gave up hope of finding.

For readers not as familiar with what has been legitimately described as pandemic drug consumption, let us begin with a few pertinent facts. In the first place, people of Earth spend more money on drugs than they spend on food, clothing, education or any social service. Between opiates, amphetamines and psychotropic substances, more than 200 million

"One is offering a person his life" —L. Ron Hubbard

men, women and children regularly consume illicit drugs and they inhabit every conceivable quarter. Indeed, the popular conception of furtive addicts haunting inner-city shooting galleries is something of a myth. The majority of those abusing drugs are employed, and they know neither geographic nor socioeconomic bounds. They are American, European, Asian and African, and they come from all over the political pie chart. To at least keep the lid on, upwards of 400 billion dollars is spent on enforcement, prevention and treatment—but it's a drop in the bucket compared to what drug abuse costs in terms of lost productivity, criminality and general mayhem. Then, too, of course, what cost the suffering?

If we have not yet specifically cited consumption of licit pharmaceuticals, including obscenely profitable psychiatric drugs, it does not mean the trade is irrelevant. Indeed, in light of legal psychotropic consumption (prescribed by physicians earning airline travel miles for every prescription written), the so-called war on illicit drugs becomes something of a joke. By way of a few particulars: consumption of psychotropics now surpasses all illegal opiates and stimulants. Meanwhile, antidepressants alone generate in excess of fifty billion annual dollars for what is aptly described as a "fast mood industry," marketing drugs for "lifestyle disorders" that are literally voted into existence by a show of psychiatric hands. Then there are the equally profitable (and potent) methylphenidates doled out to school-age

the physiological breakdown attendant to drug use is generally known, he tells us, the mental and emotional breakdown is not. In particular, and this well in advance of clinical studies on psychopharmacological violence: "Drugs can apparently change the attitude of a person

"Drugs can apparently change the attitude of a person from his original personality to one secretly harboring hostilities and hatreds he does not permit to show on the surface."

children for learning disorders that were likewise invented as part of the marketing campaign. So, yes, with a multibillion-dollar sales pitch to ram home the central message of all drug consumption—"Better Living through Chemistry"—pharmaceuticals are very definitely part of the problem. Moreover, while Zyprexa remains one of the bestselling drugs in pharmaceutical history, projected profits for later-generation antidepressants are expected to beat all records. Because, after all, populations have now been *conditioned* to swallow mood-altering drugs.

Needless to say, the ramifications are immense—and all the more so in light of L. Ron Hubbard's discoveries. For example, if

from his original personality to one secretly harboring hostilities and hatreds he does not permit to show on the surface."

That he was right (and even microscopic print on psychotropic warning labels now points to the fact) is only too obvious. To cite but a few telltale signs: there have been more than seventy pharmaceutically sparked homicides since the massive marketing of psychotherapeutics—and not a one of them discriminate. Meaning: we are now discussing drug-enraged killers who slaughter complete strangers for no conceivable reason at all. There was a fivefold increase of teenage student violence since the introduction of methylphenidates—a drug described by the United States Drug Enforcement Agency as patently precipitating violent behavior. Then there is the fact those on psychotropic drugs within correctional facilities are three to four hundred times more likely to threaten/maim than their unmedicated inmates. While if only to cap it: studies of drug-induced criminality from

to resolve what drugs represent as a spiritual stumbling block to those entering Scientology and begins with the now famed Purification Program. A carefully designed regimen of nutritional supplements, exercise and sauna, the program is universally hailed as the *only*

"The drug scene is planetwide. It is swimming in blood and human misery."

a new generation of sedative-hypnotics pointed to a "Dr. Jekyll and Mr. Hyde" effect, i.e., subjects exhibited sudden and radical personality shifts toward criminal behavior. Moreover, and even more to the point of clinical conclusions, "Their crimes were extremely violent."

One could cite much more: the appalling brutality of African/Asian "boy soldiers" has likewise been linked to psychotropic drugs, while stores of hypnotics were allegedly found in Mideast terrorist encampments and presumably used to condition suicide bombers. But L. Ron Hubbard's own concluding point hardly needs additional exposition: *"The drug scene is planetwide. It is swimming in blood and human misery."*

In reply, however, and on a commensurately global scale, he has provided his technology for drug rehabilitation. It was originally developed

means of eliminating residual drug particles and toxins from fatty tissues. That fatty tissues form a repository for drugs and toxic substances is, of course, another L. Ron Hubbard discovery and eventually led to much of what we now know as environmental medicine. It further led to a new appreciation of how drugs may affect users years after ingestion and why the problem is by no means limited to illicit substances. To be sure, both medicinal drugs and pollutants are found to lodge in fatty tissues and, as we shall see, the removal of such residues proves entirely miraculous.

The second aspect of L. Ron Hubbard's answer to drugs utilizes rehabilitation procedures drawn directly from Dianetics and Scientology. It is predicated on the fact that drugs are ultimately and invariably a problem of the mind and spirit. Accordingly, here are procedures to alleviate the mental and spiritual anguish attendant to drug usage—the scrambled thinking, the diminished awareness and, most critically of all, the underlying reason one took drugs in the first place. Those inclined to disregard a spiritual solution to physical addiction will find the full explanation of these procedures most revealing; for here, in all truth, is the only way to unburden an addict from what fuels worldwide drug abuse, i.e., *need*.

In addition to further discussion of L. Ron Hubbard's rehabilitation procedures, we shall examine the global network of Narconon centers exclusively utilizing those procedures—and, in consequence, enjoying the singularly highest success rate in the field. We shall further examine L. Ron Hubbard's work in the larger historical context of Western civilization and what he identified as a psychopolitical force behind drug proliferation. Then again, we shall examine what drugs have spawned in the way of uncommon criminality—whether subhuman or inhuman, but unspeakably violent. As a final introductory word, however, let us emphasize that L. Ron Hubbard was not simply adding to the rhetoric when decrying drugs as the "single most destructive element in these societies today." On the contrary, he has penetrated the problem, defined the solution and, in consequence, we may now proceed under the subhead: this is how L. Ron Hubbard viewed what he called the "brutal truths" of drugs, and here is what he did about it. ■

CHAPTER ONE

The Psychopolitics OF DRUG ABUSE

The Psychopolitics
of Drug Abuse

MONG THE EARLIEST LRH NOTES ON SUBSTANCE ABUSE
is a series of 1950 observations from the first disclosed cases of
United States Government drug experimentation. The story
is a fascinating one, and particularly so if we view such experimentation
as a Pandora's box from which sprang all psychedelia and the bulk of
subsequent drug usage. Yet however one accounts for modern drug abuse, those 1950 notes are extremely pertinent and do much to explain why L. Ron Hubbard's grasp of the problem was said to have been all-embracing.

Remembered today as the case of Dorothy "Dot" Jones, the critical sequence was as follows: Not long after the development of Dianetics, an inordinately distraught young woman was delivered to the LRH office in Elizabeth, New Jersey. Described as an all-but-inaccessible case, symptoms included a manic pacing about the room while repeatedly muttering, "I'm the top dog around here. I'm in the saddle." In reply, the patient was transferred to a Virginia institution (then relying exclusively on Dianetics procedures). As a word on what ensued, it might be noted that, some months earlier, with assistance from Michigan physician Dr. Joseph Winter, Ron had examined a wide array of stimulants and depressants in search of a biochemical aid to the recovery of memory. Those familiar with narcosynthesis will recognize the form, and while all drug use was finally condemned as both inhibitive of Dianetics and destructive of the personality in general, the payoff in terms of techniques to unravel the case of Dot Jones proved invaluable.

The broad strokes are these: wife of an army intelligence officer, the woman had been drugged, electroshocked and hypnotized in a willful effort at behavioral control—mind control as we know it today, pain-drug-hypnosis (PDH) as Ron would term it. As another relevant word, it might be mentioned that this pain-drug-hypnosis would finally claim several

Until the discoveries of L. Ron Hubbard, the black art of mind control had been out of sight, unsuspected and unknown

hundred victims from the periphery of the American intelligence community, allegedly including World War II pinup girl Candy Jones. It is also a factor in the disturbing case files of Robert Kennedy assassin Sirhan Sirhan. That Dianetics proved the only effective antidote to the process would prove significant on several accounts and especially as regards later federal scrutiny of LRH and his organization. But

more to the immediate point was the greater pattern of abuse revealed through succeeding cases encountered between June of 1950 and the spring of 1951.

In hindsight, of course, we now recognize the footprints of a highly extensive psychiatric-intelligence effort to devise a means of dominating human will. Variously conducted under code names Bluebird, Chatter, Artichoke and the MKULTRA umbrella, federal mind-control programs finally involved the testing of psychotropic compounds on several thousand United States citizens. The tales of abuse are legion, horrific and ultimately comparable only to medical experimentation on inmates of Nazi concentration camps (which, in fact, provided much inspiration for what took place beneath the mind-control banner). There are cases on record, more than a few, wherein unwitting victims were slipped massive doses of psychotropic drugs and effectively left to reason for themselves. Victims were also subjected to "special interrogation"

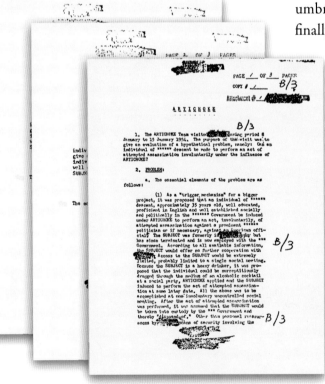

under near-fatal combinations of barbiturates and stimulants, then bombarded with ultrahigh frequency "amnesia beams." Then again, there are the cases of tortured and lobotomized victims (also to effect a memory erasure) and those subjected to elaborate psychotropic conditioning in the name of shaping the perfect killer. But the fact remains—and it is an especially significant one—that until the publication of L. Ron Hubbard's second Dianetics text, *Science of Survival,* in 1951, the black art of mind control had been "out of sight, unsuspected and unknown."

The statement cannot be overemphasized. Notwithstanding all subsequent histories of the United States mind-control effort, including Walter Bowart's *Operation Mind Control,* John D. Marks' *The Search for the "Manchurian Candidate,"* and *Acid Dreams* (Martin Lee and Bruce Shlain) nothing predated what is found in *Science of Survival:*

"There is another form of hypnotism which falls between the surgical operation and straight hypnotism without physical pain. This form of hypnotism has been a carefully guarded secret of certain military and intelligence organizations. It is a vicious war weapon and may be of considerable more use in conquering a society than the atom bomb. This is no exaggeration. The extensiveness of the use of this form of hypnotism in espionage work is so wide today that it is long past the time when people should have become alarmed about it. It required Dianetic processing to uncover 'pain-drug-hypnosis.'"

Subsequent remarks were just as pointed, and particularly so with revelations as to the potency of psychotropics employed in the name of mind control. "Now, not to scare you but to inform you," read a 1955 LRH bulletin to professional Scientologists, "psychiatry has armed itself with several new drugs. One of these, LSD, has the total goal of driving persons insane for fifteen to twenty-five hours." That a full decade would pass before

LSD became anything approaching a headline drug, much less the dark and mythic potion of the latter 1960s, is once more significant; for yet again, we find an LRH warning well in advance of general alarms. But what matters here, and what even Ron could not have anticipated, was the eventual psychedelic leakage into the cultural mainstream.

If the story has been told, the critical details are still worth repeating. Among other

"There is another form of hypnotism which falls between the surgical operation and straight hypnotism without physical pain.... The extensiveness of the use of this form of hypnotism in espionage work is so wide today that it is long past the time when people should have become alarmed about it."

celebrated champions of psychedelia to receive a first taste of "acid" through CIA-sponsored testing facilities was *The Doors of Perception* author Aldous Huxley, Grateful Dead lyricist Robert Hunter, counterculture novelist Ken Kesey and LSD high priest Richard Alpert. Then again, one finds an Agency hand in the psychedelicizing of Henry Luce—who, in turn, enticed millions with hallucinogenic spreads in *Life* magazine and so inspired none other than Timothy Leary to set out in search (literally) of the "magic mushroom." Finally, let us not forget what United States agency first enlisted Eli Lilly to synthesize lysergic acid for mass production and—lest the point has been missed—first coined the word "trip" to describe the hallucinogenic experience.

Beyond the mid-1960s, the irony runs even deeper, with what amounted to an Agency listening post in the psychedelic principality of San Francisco's Haight-Ashbury—here, among other substances supplied by Agency contract psychiatrist Louis "Jolly" West, unwitting flower children were systematically reduced to hysterics with doses of a superpsychedelic BZ. (BZ was the same agent later used with such equally devastating effects on Viet Cong irregulars by members of the First Cavalry Airmobile.) Meanwhile Agency analysts at the Rand Corporation in Santa Monica contemplated the sociopolitical repercussions of four million American youths on LSD, even as some 15 percent of all American soldiers returning from Vietnamese combat zones suffered from addiction to heroin—grown, processed and shipped into Saigon by Agency-backed syndicates.

In retrospect, it is probably difficult to appreciate how quickly the '60s soured

beyond 1967. Although street lore from the period tended to blame an infusion of heroin, methamphetamine and impure LSD—all supposedly from organized crime—one can hardly hold the Mafia accountable for what marked 1968 in terms of broad social upheaval and unmitigated violence. To cite but two telling figures: while felonious crime rates commenced a three-decade climb to historically unprecedented levels, 125 American cities erupted with riots and more than four thousand politically motivated bombings. Then, too, there is this to consider: although military-backed psychiatric experimentation failed to isolate that means of shaping the perfect killer, the hallucinogenic spillover into the streets of San Francisco had everything to do with the shaping of mass murderer Charles Manson.

"Oh, Lord," Ron was said to have exclaimed when apprised of United States usage rates circa 1968, "time has caught up with us."

After seven years in the south of England, 1968 found L. Ron Hubbard aboard his research vessel, *Apollo (below),* in the Mediterranean. It was here he wrote of the drug user living in a composite reality.

He then went on to describe his vantage point as somewhat remote. After seven years in the south of England, 1968 found him in and around the Mediterranean aboard his famed research vessel, *Apollo,* where even the more cosmopolitan ports of call in Spain and Portugal would not feel the psychedelic tidal wave for several years to come. Moreover, his crew, drawn from the world of Scientology, was wholly drug-free and so it was not until

continued growth of the Church brought commensurate needs for more hands that he even glimpsed that notoriously strange Class of '68.

As a preliminary observation, he described the former user as delusory, inattentive and prone to "blank" periods—all, incidentally, accounted for within the psychedelic lexicon as "spaced-out," "zoned-out" and "out of it." He additionally noted a marked weakness in both written and verbal comprehension as well as sorely deficient communication skills. Then, too, he spoke of the user as living in a "composite reality," with no distinction between past and present and otherwise exhibiting behavior with real parallels to insanity. Finally, and herein lay the primary point of LRH concern, the former user proved utterly incapable of spiritual advancement through Scientology.

The problem would prove insidious, considerable and complex. But for the moment let us focus upon what he described as

the biochemical barrier to mental and spiritual advancement, and specifically as regards LSD. Again, a word on the irony is appropriate. After all, here was the original psychiatric ticket to altered states and expanded consciousness, the key to those legendary doors of perception at only five bucks a hit. The catch, however, were veritable scars on the soul that proved all but permanent.

To explain: In addition to the more immediate action of LSD—in fact involving nothing more than a constriction of blood vessels to the cerebral cortex—was the drug's curious tendency to occasionally reactivate. A *flashback,* it is termed on the street and may involve full-blown hallucinatory experiences years after ingestion. Also noted within LRH papers of the period was that peculiar sense of disassociation common to the LSD user—"dead in the head," to once more cite the lexicon, and with "eyes that looked like blank discs," as Ron himself so pointedly phrased it. Then followed certain very pertinent questions on the action of such drugs upon the central nervous system, while he simultaneously examined what "acid" spawned in terms of '70s pharmaceutical usage. Finally, we find him tracking the larger sociological consequences of such usage, bolstered on by that multibillion-dollar pharmaceutical promotion—until, at last, we come upon this chilling description of psychotropic users: "They are dehumanized and can be vicious or irrationally cruel." ∎

In what amounts to a policy statement on the role of Scientology to rid this world of drug abuse comes L. Ron Hubbard's "Drug Problems." It dates from September of 1969, or when the first body of his drug rehabilitation technology was under pilot in recovery centers across the United States and Europe. That so many young people then entering Scientology had previously taken drugs was, of course, a sign of the times (the Summer of Love only recently turning chilly and a "Purple Haze" still clouding campuses). On the other hand, and by actual survey, Scientologists are entirely free of drug abuse.

DRUG PROBLEMS

by L. Ron Hubbard

I N AT LEAST TWO countries, Scientology is closely cooperating with the government in programs to handle the drug addiction problem now becoming chronic in society.

Drug addicts have been found to have begun drug taking because of physical suffering or hopelessness.

In one country a Scientology pilot project has been in progress for about a year and has produced data of great value. Even without processing, but by education, some 50 percent of the committed addicts have recovered and have not been recommitted.

By eradicating in the addict the cause of the original suffering or hopelessness, the need of drugs is voluntarily dispensed with by the former addict.

These Scientology projects are pilot in nature and were undertaken to develop the programs for larger applications. At present the number of unselected cases number only a few hundred.

So far it has been found that the cost per case, exclusive of food and bed, is about £35 a person when done on a mass basis using individual practitioners. The time is between seven and ten weeks, the first six of which are spent "drying out" under medical care. The actual processing takes less than fifty hours to permanent full rehabilitation. If only the drug factor is handled, the time is under ten hours.

A pilot project has just been begun in a state prison where the addicts will be trained to handle one another's cases. If successful, this could greatly reduce costs and facilitate the handling of very large numbers.

The addict has been found not to want to be an addict, but is driven by pain and environmental hopelessness.

As soon as an addict can feel healthier and more competent mentally and physically without drugs than he does on drugs, he ceases to require drugs.

Drug addiction has been shrugged off by psychiatry as "unimportant" and the social problem of drug taking has received no attention from psychiatrists—rather the contrary, since they themselves introduced and popularized LSD. And many of them are pushers.

"The addict has been found not to want to be an addict, but is driven by pain and environmental hopelessness."

Government agencies have failed markedly to halt the increase in drug taking and there has been no real or widespread cure.

The political implications of increasing addiction in a country are great. All nations under heavy attack by foreign intelligence agencies have experienced increased drug traffic and addiction.

Japanese intelligence forces before World War II conquered by carefully making addicts out of every potential leader they could reach, particularly bright children, in a target country.

The last dynasty (the Manchu) of China was overthrown by a country that imported opium into the kingdom and got it into widespread use.

There are many historical precedents.

The liability of the drug user, even after he has ceased to use drugs, is that he "goes blank" at unexpected times, has periods of irresponsibility and tends to sicken easily.

Dianetics and Scientology processing has been able to eradicate the major damage in those cases tested as well as make further addiction unnecessary and unwanted.

Scientology has no interest in the political or social aspects of the various types of drugs or even drug taking as such. The whole interest of Scientology is concentrated on those who want to "get unhooked" and "stay unhooked."

In one Scientology organization at least half of those coming in for processing have been on drugs and this figure is less than that in the surrounding public, where it evidently goes to an even higher percentage. Therefore in 1968 and 1969 research on this as a specialized subject was completed successfully.

Scientologists do not stand ready to punish drug takers or reform a whole society on the subject. But they do stand ready and are active in helping anyone or any government to handle the problem.

Like the Flaming Youth era of the Prohibition 20s, drug taking will probably also come to pass away as a national pastime. But it will leave a lot of people who wish they hadn't. The Scientologists can help those. And are helping them right now as a routine duty to the community.

Governments need the Scientologist a lot more than they think.

"Like the Flaming Youth era of the Prohibition 20s, drug taking will probably also come to pass away as a national pastime. But it will leave a lot of people who wish they hadn't. The Scientologists can help those. And are helping them right now as a routine duty to the community."

Central to the rehabilitation methods of L. Ron Hubbard is a deeply religious view of Man as intrinsically spiritual, potentially omnipotent and ultimately capable of resolving all that afflicts him. Or as LRH himself so succinctly phrased it: "The only truly therapeutic agent in this universe is the spirit." Beneath that statement are the axiomatic truths of Dianetics and Scientology, including recognition that physical and emotional health is solely dependent upon spiritual well-being.

Conversely, however, if Man is merely the hodgepodge of his physical parts and his emotional stability is strictly determined by brain chemistry, then a Brave New World of drug consumption becomes de rigueur.

The point is pivotal and bears upon the whole pharmaceutical sales pitch for sinfully profitable psychotropic drugs. It also bears upon replacement treatment wherein one addictive drug is substituted for another (frequently even more addictive). Then again, it bears upon those annual billions in psychopharmacological advertising to convince us we are imperfect beings by nature, so let us alter that nature by adjusting the chemistry. The rub, of course, is an international drug crisis that is absolutely unique in human history and arguably rivals the Black Death in terms of cultural waste.

Such is the perspective, then, from which L. Ron Hubbard addresses "Drug Addiction." It dates from October 1969, or on the heels of his research to unravel the mental and spiritual underpinnings of addiction.

DRUG ADDICTION

by L. RON HUBBARD

IN THE ABSENCE OF workable psychotherapy, wide drug addiction is inevitable.

When a person is depressed or in pain and where he finds no physical relief from treatment, he will eventually discover for himself that drugs remove his symptoms.

In almost all cases of psychosomatic pain, malaise or discomfort, the person has sought some cure for the upset.

When he at last finds that only drugs give him relief, he will surrender to them and become dependent upon them, often to the point of addiction.

Years before, had there been any other way out, most people would have taken it. But when they are told there is no cure, that their pains are "imaginary," life tends to become insupportable. They then can become chronic drug takers and are in danger of addiction.

The time required to make an addict varies, of course. The complaint itself may only be "sadness" or "weariness." The ability to confront life, in any case, is reduced.

Any substance that brings relief or makes life less a burden physically or mentally will then be welcome.

In an unsettled and insecure environment, psychosomatic illness is very widespread.

So before any government strikes too heavily at spreading drug use, it should recognize that it is a symptom of failed psychotherapy. The social scientist, the psychologist and psychiatrist and health ministries have failed to handle spreading psychosomatic illness.

It is too easy to blame it all on "social unrest" or "the pace of modern society."

The hard, solid fact is that there has been no effective psychotherapy in broad practice. The result is a drug-addicted population.

Dianetics was designed as broadly applicable low-cost mental health. It is the only mental technology fully validated by actual test. It is fast. It is effective.

Health services should assist it into wide general use.

It can handle the problem. *₢—*

"The hard, solid fact is that there has been
no effective psychotherapy in broad practice.
The result is a drug-addicted population."

CHAPTER TWO

Purification
PROGRAM

Purification
Program

"THE SOCIETY HAS BECOME, BY ALL EVIDENCE TO HAND, A biochemical problem." —L. Ron Hubbard

Given the tendency of LSD to reactivate long after ingestion and given even minute dosages can trigger reactivation, L. Ron Hubbard finally deduced that LSD residue must stay in the system. The statement is far more momentous than one might immediately imagine, particularly with a correlative discovery that all toxic substances—preservatives, pesticides and the full array of both street and medicinal drugs—may likewise lodge in fatty tissues and wreak havoc.

Such was the investigatory trail eventually culminating in the development of the Purification Program. In simplest terms, the program may be described as deep and long-range detoxification. If originally designed to eliminate biochemical barriers to Scientology services, the medical and scientific community were quick to take note. After all, here was the first positive means of flushing not only drug residues, but environmental toxins—and results were both clinically measurable and highly dramatic. As an overriding word, Ron tells us that while residues may seriously disturb fluid balances and more, the primary focus of the Purification Program lies with the actual residues themselves and interconnected mental phenomena.

How exactly drug and toxin deposits interplay with the human thinking process, and how the Purification Program eliminates those deposits is the subject of Ron's original description of the program as reprinted here. By way of further background, however, the following may be of interest:

"Over the past few years, private research firms working in cooperation with government scientists in studying the Hubbard method of detoxification have concluded that the pioneering efforts of its developer, author and researcher L. Ron Hubbard, were in fact valid. While the technique has been widely acclaimed, only in recent years have environmental scientists documented its effectiveness as a means of coming to grips with the myriad of chemical-exposure-related problems now facing modern society." —Robert B. Amidon, *Journal of California Law Enforcement*.

By way of example come conclusions drawn from a now famous study of Michigan residents exposed to polybrominated biphenyls (PBBs) following a statewide contamination of fire-retardant in livestock feed. Given stored residues of PBBs (and related polychlorinated biphenyls from industrial coolants) will naturally reduce but half in ten to twenty years, reduction rates from the Purification Program proved entirely startling. On the average, those Michigan residents entering the program saw an immediate 20 percent reduction of chemical residues, while four-month follow-up examinations revealed a full 40 percent reduction. That toxic reduction continued well after the program's completion was also, of course, deemed significant but not unique to the Michigan study. Indeed, a Florida study of a patient exposed to dioxin, a toxic byproduct of herbicide manufacture, found an immediate reduction of 29 percent after completion of the Purification Program, with a further reduction of 97 percent approximately eight months later.

That such reductions translate into greater health and well-being is likewise unequivocal. United States military personnel exposed to the herbicide-defoliant Agent Orange, for example, routinely complained of fatigue, insomnia, abdominal pains, headaches and persistent skin ailments—all of which resolved through the course of the Purification Program. Similarly resolved was much of what characterized "Vietnam Syndrome" in the way of cyclical depression and rage. Results proved equally dramatic in the resolution of "Gulf War Syndrome" and particularly those exposed to anti-nerve-gas biological-warfare agents.

Program results from New York's Ground Zero proved just as telling. Police, fire, medical emergency and rescue teams were afforded the program after exposure to unprecedented levels of toxic dust, fume and vapor in the wake of the World Trade Center collapse. In a word, the recovery from insomnia, exhaustion and a respiratory ailment colloquially known as the "WTC Cough" was nothing short of miraculous. Indeed, many a previously ailing rescue worker told of rejuvenation above and beyond 9/11 quality of life. That is—and this from the Senior Medical Advisor—"They actually feel better than they did before the attacks." Hence the eventual government funding of the New

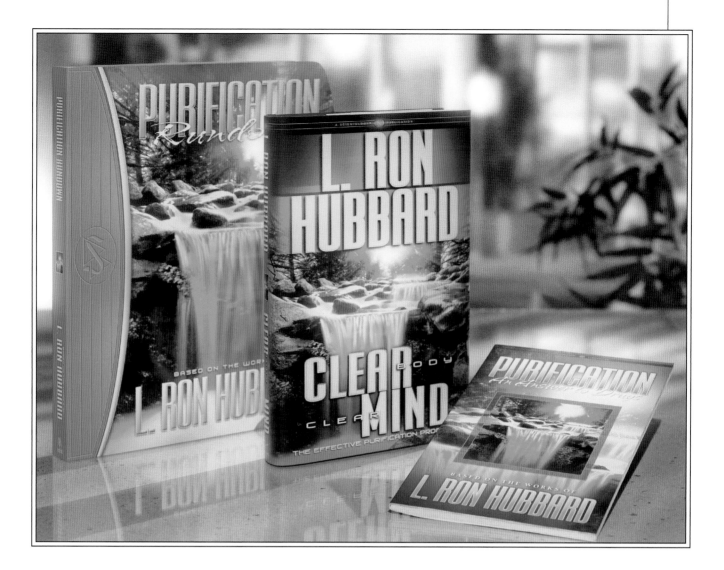

York Rescue Workers Detoxification Project and that Senior Medical Advisor's conclusory report: *"We are returning to families the mothers and fathers that the dust of 9/11 had seemed to swallow."*

Among those exposed to "acceptable" levels of environmental toxins—which is to say, pollutant levels in any urban setting—the recommendation is equally unqualified. Included in the measurable gains: improved vitality, memory, concentration and, apparently a consequence of food additives, relief from long-term abdominal/intestinal pain. No less significant are the reports of improved mental outlook and emotional stability—all suggesting that even relatively low levels of toxic residues from atmospheric pollutants may affect behavior and block clear thinking.

Yet to appreciate just how acutely such residues may alter behavior and thinking, let us refocus on drugs. As noted, the impact of drugs and drug residues upon behavior and perception is considerable. Among the mass of sociological literature regularly offered up in explanation of post-'60s substance abuse was a relatively obscure 1972 examination of New York City heroin addicts as "reshaped" through the psychedelic revolution. The central premise, and then a radical one: "A new and different breed of heroin user was living on the streets of American cities." A descendant of multiple-drug users from 1967 and 1968, this late twentieth-century addict was said to have been wholly indiscriminate, i.e., he would take what he could get from both illicit heroin trade and, even more significantly, street sales

Above
L. Ron Hubbard's research and discoveries concerning drugs and toxins, their effects on an individual, and the Purification Program are described in the above three books

of regularly prescribed pharmaceuticals. In consequence, and this in contrast to earlier portraits of a relatively peaceable addict, he was shockingly violent.

are chilling. Could it be, proposed New York's Narcotic and Drug Research Inc., that we are facing a "systemic model" of drug-related crime wherein violence is actually intrinsic to usage?

"The society has become, by all evidence to hand, a biochemical problem."

Subsequent investigation confirmed it. A principal study of the heroin user in Dade County, Florida, found a selection of 573 addicts committing 215,105 criminal offenses through the course of a single year. True, approximately half were "victimless" crimes, primarily prostitution and trafficking. Yet also cited were some six thousand robberies and assaults, more than a few of an extreme and unreasonable nature. A second study revealed the same and worse: in any twelve-month period 356 users committed 120,000 crimes, including homicides, robberies, forcible rapes and aggravated assaults. Moreover, 78 percent of those convicted of a violent crime were regular users and a significant number of those crimes were not even in support of habits. Rather, victims were murdered, raped and beaten at random and for no logical reason at all.

Conclusions, even from a sociological community cautious of blanket deductions,

In partial answer came the equally chilling model of violent behavior as exhibited by those using licit psychotropic drugs. As noted, a 1975 Canadian study found inmates of correctional facilities far more likely to commit acts of violence when medicated with psychotropic drugs; while so violent were the episodes on sedative-hypnotics, researchers pointed to that "Dr. Jekyll and Mr. Hyde" effect. Then, too, among other frequently discussed side effects of antidepressants is an irritability factor and anxiety quotient—phrases which become absurdly euphemistic when considering the likes of an Ilo Grundberg, who butchered her eighty-three-year-old mother in what can only be described as a psychotropic rage. (The woman was actually acquitted of charges after prosecutors failed to establish any conceivable motive for a murder she did not even remember committing.) Meanwhile, adverse reactions from the Prozac file suggest even nastier definitions of the label warning for anxiety—as in the now infamous case of Joseph Wesbecker, who entered his former workplace with therapeutic levels of the drug in his blood and mowed down twenty victims with an assault rifle.

One could mention many another: the schoolyard-shooting spree at Colorado's Columbine High School was masterminded by a psychotropically enraged student, as were teenage killings in Oregon, Mississippi and Georgia. But the greater point is merely this: just over a century ago, as sociologists are prone to remind us, Jack the Ripper shocked civilized society with the murder of seven English prostitutes. As we embark through this new millennium, we seem to encounter Jack the Ripper every two or three years—and he is invariably on one or more psychotropics.

Such is the larger perspective from which L. Ron Hubbard declared, "The society has become, by all evidence to hand, a biochemical problem." He then proceeded to cite both correlative mayhem and a general moral crisis, and so presented his solution. It is simple enough to apply, absolutely intended for broad use and, in a very candid statement of fact, he wishes us to know it is our only hope. ■

THE PURIFICATION PROGRAM

by L. RON HUBBARD

WE LIVE IN A chemical-oriented society.

One would be hard put to find someone in the present-day civilization who is not affected by this fact. Every day the vast majority of the public is subjected to the intake of food preservatives and other chemical poisons, including atmospheric poisons and pesticides. Added to this are the pain pills, tranquilizers, psychiatric and other medical drugs prescribed by doctors. Additionally the widespread use of marijuana, LSD, cocaine and other street drugs contribute heavily to the scene.

These factors are *all* part of the biochemical problem.

BIOCHEMICAL means the interaction of life forms and chemical substances.

BIO- means life, of living things; from the Greek *bios,* life or way of life.

CHEMICAL means of or having to do with chemicals. Chemicals are substances, simple or complex, that are the building blocks of matter.

The human body is composed of certain exact chemicals and chemical compounds, with complex chemical processes going on continuously within it. Some substances, such as nutrients, air and water, are vital to the continuation of these processes and for maintaining the body's health. Other substances are relatively neutral when entered into the body, causing neither benefit nor damage. Still other substances can wreak havoc, blocking or perverting body functions and making the body ill or even killing it.

TOXIC SUBSTANCES, which fall into this last category, are those that upset the body's normal chemical balance or interfere with its processes. The term is used to describe drugs, chemicals or any substance shown to be poisonous or harmful to an organism. The word *toxic* itself comes from the Greek word *toxikon,* which originally meant a poison in which arrows were dipped.

DETOXIFICATION would be the action of removing a poison or a poisonous effect from something, such as from one's body.

Toxins in Abundance

An enormous volume of material has been written on the subject of toxic substances, their reported effects and the prospects for their handling. Examples abound in publications and news reports.

The current environment is permeated with life-hostile elements. Drugs, radioactive wastes, pollutants and chemical agents of all types are not only everywhere, but are becoming even more prevalent as time goes on. In fact, they are so commonplace they are almost impossible to avoid.

For example, some of the things put in canned vegetables or soup could be considered toxic. They are preservatives and the action of a preservative is to impede decay. Yet digestion and cellular action are based on decay. In other words, those things might be great for the manufacturer, as they preserve the product, *but* they could be very bad for the consumer. It is not that I am on a food faddism kick or a kick against preservatives. The point is that Man is surrounded by toxins.

This example alone of preservatives in foods illustrates the degree to which one can encounter toxic substances in daily living.

But combine that with the enemies of various countries using widespread drug addiction as a defeatist mechanism and nations vying with each other in the manufacture and testing of nuclear weapons (and so increasing the amount of radioactive material free in the environment). Then add the ready availability of painkillers and sedatives, the increased use of industrial and agricultural

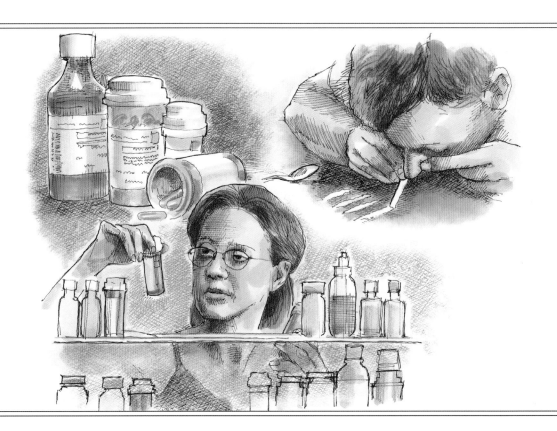

Drugs are essentially poisons. The degree to which they are taken determines the effect.

chemicals, and toxic substances developed for chemical warfare. In short (and putting it bluntly), this society, at this time, is riddled with toxic substances.

Certain data regarding those substances that pose a threat to individuals and to society at large will bring the biochemical situation more clearly into focus. It is to this situation that the Purification Program is addressed.

Drugs

Drugs are essentially poisons. The degree to which they are taken determines the effect. A small amount acts as a stimulant (increases activity). A greater amount acts as a sedative (suppresses activity). A larger amount acts as a poison and can kill one dead.

This is true of any drug and each has a different amount at which it gives those results. Caffeine is a drug, so coffee is an example. One hundred cups of coffee would probably kill a person. Ten cups would probably put him to sleep. Two or three cups stimulates. This is a very common drug. It is not very harmful, as it takes so much of it to have an effect. So it is known as a stimulant.

Arsenic is a known poison. Yet a tiny amount of arsenic is a stimulant, a larger dose puts one to sleep and a few grains kill.

Street Drugs

The drug scene is planetwide and swimming in blood and human misery.

Research demonstrates that the single most destructive element present in our current culture is drugs.

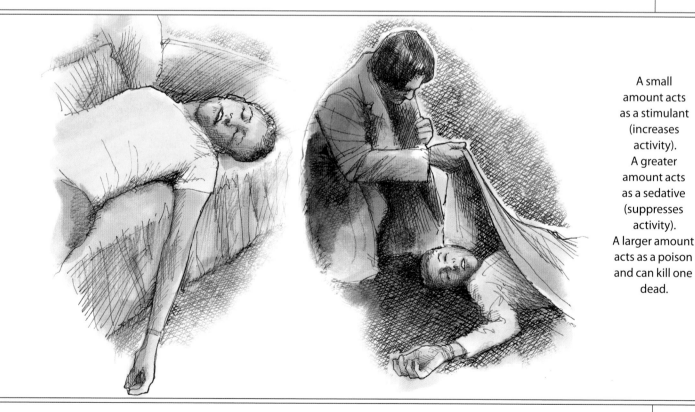

A small amount acts as a stimulant (increases activity). A greater amount acts as a sedative (suppresses activity). A larger amount acts as a poison and can kill one dead.

The acceleration of widespread use of drugs such as LSD, heroin, cocaine, marijuana and the litany of new street drugs all play a part in our debilitated society. Even schoolchildren are shoved onto drugs. And children of drug-taking mothers are born as druggies.

Reportedly some of these drugs can cause brain and nerve damage. Marijuana, for example, so favored by college students, who are supposed to be getting bright today so they can be the executives of tomorrow, is reported capable of causing brain atrophy.

Research even established that there is such a thing as a "drug personality." It is artificial and is created by drugs. Drugs can apparently change the attitude of persons from their original personality to one secretly harboring hostilities and hatreds they do not permit to show on the surface. While this may not hold true in all cases, it does establish a link between drugs and increasing difficulties with crime, failing productivity and the modern breakdown of social and industrial culture.

The devastating physiological effects of drugs are the subject of newspaper headlines routinely. That they also result in a breakdown of mental alertness and ethical fiber is all too obvious.

But vicious and damaging though they are, street drugs are actually only one part of the biochemical problem.

Medical and Psychiatric Drugs

Medical and, most particularly, the long list of psychiatric drugs (Ritalin, Valium, Thorazine and lithium, to name a few) can be every bit as damaging as street drugs. The prevalence of these currently in common use would be quite amazing to one unfamiliar with the problem.

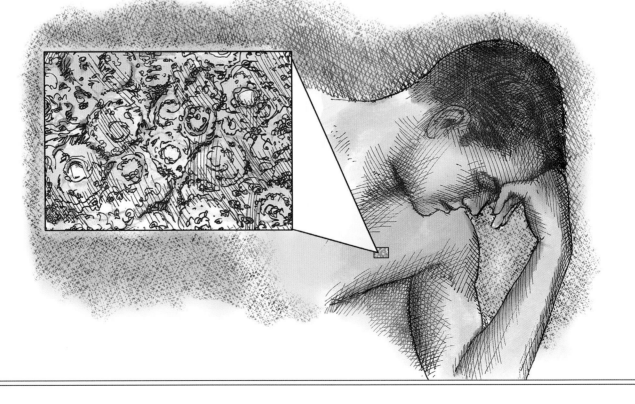

In the course of L. Ron Hubbard's research into the inhibiting effects of drugs upon an individual's spiritual advance, he made a startling discovery: LSD residues can lodge in the body, mainly the fatty tissues, and remain there for years.

Sedatives are often administered as though they were a panacea for all ills. As early as 1951, many persons had become so accustomed to their daily dosage of sleeping pills or painkillers that they did not consider their "little pills" as drugs.

Too often the attitude is "If I can't find the cause of the pain, at least I'll deaden it." In the case of one who is mentally ill, this might read, "If he can't be made rational, at least he can be made quiet."

Unfortunately it is not recognized that a person whose pain has been deadened by a sedative has himself been deadened by the same drug and is much nearer the ultimate pain of death. It should be obvious that the quietest people in the world are the dead.

Alcohol

Alcohol is not a mind-altering drug, but it is a biochemical-altering drug. Alcohol doesn't do anything to the mind; it does something to the nerves. By quickly and rapidly soaking up all the vitamin B_1 in the body, it makes the nerves incapable of functioning properly.

Therefore a person can't coordinate his body. Alcohol in small quantities is a stimulant and in large quantities is a depressant.

The definition of *alcoholics* is individuals who can't have just *one* drink. If they have one drink, they have to have another. They are addicted. One of the factors is they have to have a full glass in front of them. If it gets empty, it has to be refilled.

Alcoholics are in a state of total, unrelenting hostility toward everything around them. They will do people in without even mentioning it.

These deposits can continue to adversely affect the individual long after he has stopped taking the drug. In the case of LSD, residues of the drug were found to account for the unpredictable recurrences of "flashbacks" former users experienced.

Alcohol is a drug. The degree of alcohol consumption (quantity and frequency) determines whether an individual should be considered a heavy user.

Commercial Processes and Products

In recent years much research has been done on the potential toxic effects of many of the substances commonly used in various commercial processes and products and to what extent they may find their way into the bodies of this planet's inhabitants. Following are a few examples of what this research is bringing to light.

INDUSTRIAL CHEMICALS

Under this heading exist the tens of thousands of chemicals used in manufacturing. Not all such chemicals are toxic, of course. But workers in factories that produce or use such things as pesticides, petroleum products, plastics, detergents and cleaning chemicals, solvents, plated metals, preservatives, drugs, asbestos products, fertilizers, some cosmetics, perfumes, paints, dyes, electrical equipment or any radioactive materials can be exposed, often for extended periods, to toxic materials. Of course, the consumer can be exposed to residual amounts of such chemicals when they use these products.

AGRICULTURAL CHEMICALS

Pesticides are the most obvious of the toxic substances to which workers in agricultural activities could be exposed. These include insecticides (insect-killing chemicals), herbicides (chemicals to kill unwanted plants, such as weeds) and man-made fertilizers.

Under the heading of herbicides come several that contain a substance called "dioxin," known to be a highly toxic chemical even in amounts almost too small to detect in the body.

It was discovered that deposits from marijuana, heroin, cocaine, painkillers and other medical drugs similarly can trigger into action years later, as if the person had just taken more of the drug.

Contact with chemicals used in agriculture can occur in a number of ways. The chemical can be carried on or in the plant itself and so eaten. It can be carried on the wind and breathed in directly by those living or working in agricultural areas. It can even be carried into drinking-water supplies.

FOOD, FOOD ADDITIVES AND PRESERVATIVES

There are substances added to some commercially processed foods that are meant to "enhance" color or flavor or, as mentioned previously, to keep the food from spoiling. Also becoming more common are various artificial sweeteners used in "diet" soft drinks and other commercially packaged foods. From research on these "enhancers" and "sweeteners" and "preservers," it appears that many of them are quite toxic. The whole subject of food additives and preservatives has become a matter of concern to many people.

There is another side to this matter of food. Research findings point to the possibility that rancid oils are a health hazard of a magnitude not previously suspected. Oils used in cooking or commercial processing of foods, where they are not fresh, pure and free of rancidity, have been linked, by researchers, with digestive and muscular ills and even cancer.

PERFUMES AND FRAGRANCES

Use of perfumes and fragrances in all sorts of products has become more and more prevalent in recent years. Everything from clothing and laundry detergent, to facial tissue and magazine advertisements, has fragrance added to it. That fragrance is usually a cheap chemical derivative, an extract of coal tar that probably costs about 10 cents for a 50-gallon drum. Findings seem to bear out that these chemicals, floating about in the local supermarket as "fragrances," are actually toxic and can end up in the food products sold there. Ingesting these chemicals is clearly no aid to digestion.

It is not just drugs that lodge in the body, but any of the steady stream of toxic substances we encounter every day. The accumulation of toxic deposits in the body tissues can negatively affect a person's life.

Radiation

You've no doubt seen in the news that contact with radiation can occur through exposure to nuclear weapons tests (or the radioactive particles they can release into the atmosphere), to nuclear wastes or to some manufacturing processes that use radioactive materials. Further, the increased use of atomic power for electrical supply, without developing proper technology and safeguards in its use, poses a nonmilitary threat. And the deterioration of the upper atmosphere of the planet by pollutants year by year lets more and more solar radiation through to the planetary surface.

In other words, there are many ways one can be exposed to radiation. It's all over the atmosphere and always has been. There is just more of it now.

Sun worshipers, sunbathers, those who make a career of baking themselves in the sun year after year, expose themselves to radiation. What is the Sun but a ball of radiation? No better example of radiation can be found anywhere than our own Sun; it is pure fission. Therefore a sunburn *is* a burn, but not a burn that occurs simply from excessive heat: it is a radiation burn. A certain amount of sunlight is probably essential to the good health of the human body. It is excessive exposure we are talking about here. Even when one does not burn, per se, with extensive daily exposure over long periods of time, one is subjected to the cumulative effects of radiation.

X-rays also expose one to radiation. They are fully as deadly as atomic fission. X-ray does not bring about the big bang; you don't get a tremendous explosion and no town left. But it does, X-ray by X-ray, bring about a condition of high count in the individual so that if one gets a little bit more X-ray or fallout, one is liable to become ill. A repeated, continuous application of X-ray to a person can bring about anything and everything that atomic fission brings about in its pollution of the atmosphere.

Even after quitting drugs, one retains mental image pictures of drug experiences. As long as toxic substances remain trapped in the body they can reactivate these pictures, causing negative effects.

Where there is a radioactive atmosphere, there is also a declining health rate. The more people are exposed to radiation, the less resistance they have and the more effect the radiation has on them. In other words, a buildup occurs in the body, over time, from any of the sources described above. As radiation is cumulative, it follows, then, that this compounds the biochemical problem and presents a barrier of magnitude.

An Answer to the Biochemical World

In light of all of the above, the Purification Program is a proffered answer to this biochemical problem. In a society as pervaded with drugs and toxic materials as this one has become, handling accumulations of such materials should be a point of great interest.

The logical questions regarding any procedure that might handle such accumulations would be "Does it work?" "Does it get *results?*"

These questions are answered by practical experience and through an understanding of the basic discoveries that brought about a procedure to free the individual from the harmful effects of toxic substances.

The Development of the Purification Program

With the explosion of the drug problem in the 1960s, when the use of illicit street drugs and their ravaging effects had become a dominant factor among society's ills, I developed a set of procedures called the Drug Rundown. The Drug Rundown deals directly with the mental effect of drugs that can be restimulated and affect an individual adversely. The rundown frees attention from past drug

Drugs and chemical residues can make a person feel blank, stupid, depressed, confused—for no apparent reason. They can alter one's personality for the worse and change one's attitude toward life.

incidents so people are more able to deal with life and better able to control themselves and the things in their surroundings. This rundown remains in use today as the final resolution to any drug handling.

However, in the 1970s, it became apparent that underlying factors may need to be handled prior to doing this rundown. Working with individuals who had been drug users, in a study of their physical symptoms and behavioral patterns, I made a startling discovery:

People who had been on LSD at some earlier time appeared to relapse and act as if they had just taken more LSD.

As it has been stated that it takes only one millionth of an ounce of LSD to produce a drugged condition and because LSD is basically wheat rust, which simply cuts off the circulation, my original thinking on this was that LSD must remain in the body.

The most likely place for a toxic substance to lock up is in the body's fatty tissue. It has been said that in middle age, the body's ability to break down fat decreases. So here we have, apparently, a situation of toxic substances locked up in fatty tissue and the fatty tissue is not being broken down. As a result, such toxic substances can accumulate.

In other words:

LSD APPARENTLY STAYS IN THE SYSTEM, LODGING IN THE TISSUES, MAINLY THE FATTY TISSUES OF THE BODY, AND IS LIABLE TO GO INTO ACTION AGAIN, GIVING THE PERSON UNPREDICTABLE "TRIPS" EVEN YEARS AFTER THE PERSON HAS COME OFF LSD.

Thousands of hours of research and testing culminated in the development of the Purification Program, a process by which drug and toxic residues can be eliminated from the body.

Thus the behavior, actions and responsibility level of those who had taken LSD were unpredictable! Not to mention that these "flashbacks" could be quite fatal while driving or even walking around.

What was the answer to these cases?

No known method existed for ridding the body of these minute drug deposits that, locked as they were in the tissues, were not totally dispelled in the normal processes of elimination.

The answer obviously did not lie in attempting to handle this with more drugs or biochemicals, which would only compound the situation. But could a method be evolved to dislodge and flush these deposits out, thereby freeing the person for full rehabilitation physically as well as mentally and spiritually?

The Original "Sweat Program"

In 1977, I developed and released a regimen called the "Sweat Program." It operated on the premise that the negative factors observed might be reversed if there were a means of getting LSD deposits out of the system and that the most logical method to accomplish that would be to sweat them out.

Persons on the program experienced the apparent exudation of substances other than just LSD. They reported smelling or tasting or feeling the effects of a host of other street drugs and chemicals, the same ones they had consumed or were exposed to years earlier.

They were also experiencing, in mild form, some of the sensations of old sunburns, past illnesses and injuries and other past physical and emotional conditions.

The Purification Program is an exact regimen that combines exercise, sauna sweat-out and nutrition.

Therefore it appeared that:

NOT ONLY LSD, BUT OTHER CHEMICAL POISONS AND TOXINS, PRESERVATIVES, PESTICIDES, ETC., AS WELL AS MEDICINAL DRUGS AND THE LONG LIST OF STREET DRUGS (HEROIN, MARIJUANA, COCAINE, ETC.), CAN LODGE IN THE TISSUES AND REMAIN IN THE BODY FOR YEARS.

EVEN MEDICINAL DRUGS SUCH AS DIET PILLS, CODEINE, NOVOCAIN AND OTHERS, AS WELL AS PSYCHIATRIC DRUGS, CAN BE REACTIVATED YEARS AFTER THEY WERE TAKEN AND SUPPOSEDLY HAD BEEN ELIMINATED FROM THE BODY.

Thus it seemed that any or all of these hostile biochemical substances could get caught in the tissues and their accumulation probably disarranged the biochemistry and fluid balance of the body.

This was my early thinking on the subject. It was now being borne out by further research as more and more manifestations occurred. (It has also since been borne out by clinical tests and by medical autopsies that have found deposits of certain drugs embedded in body tissues.)

Moreover, as research continued with those on the Sweat Program, all indicators were that these substances were being flushed out as people progressed on the program. And these same individuals were reporting that they felt a new vigor, a renewed vitality and interest in life.

The Sweat Program was a lengthy process, however, taking months to complete. A refinement and speed-up was needed and so I developed the Purification Program.

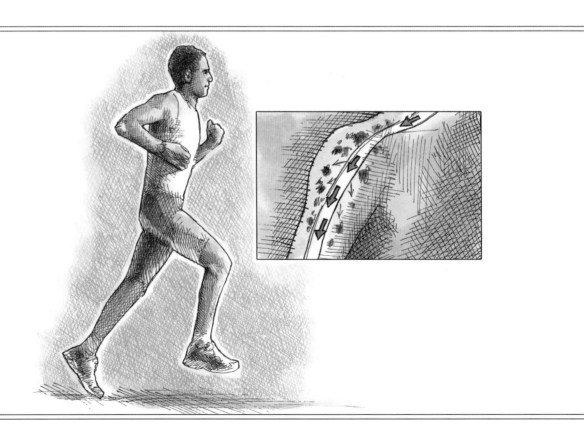

The first step of the program is running. Running gets the blood circulating faster and reaching deeper into the tissues where the harmful deposits are trapped. This helps loosen toxic residues.

Elements of the Purification Program

The Purification Program is a tightly supervised regimen that includes the following elements:

1. Exercise (running)
2. Sauna sweat-out
3. Nutrition, including vitamins, minerals, etc., as well as oil intake
4. A properly ordered personal schedule

Participants run to get the blood circulating deeper into the tissues where toxic residuals are lodged and thus to loosen and release the accumulated harmful deposits and get them moving.

It is very important, then, that the running be immediately followed by sweating in the sauna to flush out these dislodged accumulations.

While supplementing one's regular diet with plenty of fresh vegetables, one also takes an exact regimen of vitamins, minerals and extra quantities of oil. The recommended vitamin dosages are gradiently increased over the course of the program. (By *gradiently* is meant a gradual approach to something, taken step by step: in this case, a gradual increase of vitamins.) This regimen is not only a vital factor in helping the body flush out toxins, it also repairs and rebuilds areas affected by drugs and other toxic residuals.

A proper schedule with enough rest is mandatory because the body undergoes change and repair throughout the program.

These actions, carried out on a very stringently monitored basis, apparently accomplish a detoxification of the entire system, to the renewed health and vigor of the individual.

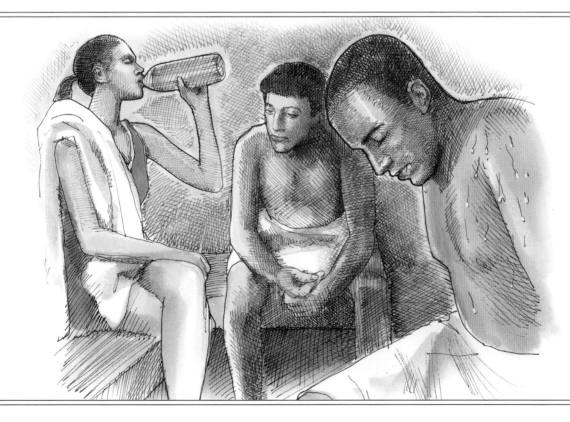

Running is immediately followed by time in the sauna. Profuse sweating allows the dislodged residues to leave the body through the pores.

Mental and Spiritual Aspects

There is, however, a more in-depth and comprehensive view to be taken of the entire process, including the mental and spiritual aspects of the program. For beyond any physical damage they may cause, many drugs—marijuana, peyote, morphine, heroin, to name but a few—have another liability: they directly affect the person's mind. As one example, LSD, originally designed for psychiatric use, can reportedly make schizophrenics out of normal people.

But to better understand these mental effects of drugs, it is necessary to know something about what the mind is.

As people go through life, their minds record pictures of everything they perceive, moment by moment, twenty-four hours a day. These *mental image pictures* are three-dimensional color pictures that contain all perceptions—all that the individual has seen, heard, felt, smelled, tasted and experienced.

The consecutive record of mental image pictures that accumulates through a person's life is called the *time track*. It is very exactly dated. Ordinarily one's time track is made up of the recorded moment-to-moment events experienced as one moves through life. However, a person who has taken drugs, in addition to the physical factors involved, retains mental image pictures of those drugs and their effects. In other words, their time track for that period is not made up of present time events only. Instead it is jumbled: their mental records and perceptions are distorted and tangled up, combining actual events, imagination and pictures from incidents in the past.

For example, let us say at some point in time an individual took LSD at an outdoor rock concert on a hot summer day. Let us further suppose that the person experienced a number of severe side effects while under the influence of the drug. These included higher body temperature, increased heart rate,

Nutrition is another key element to the program. Vitamins and minerals help repair the damage done by drug and toxic substances and assist in rebuilding the tissues and cells.

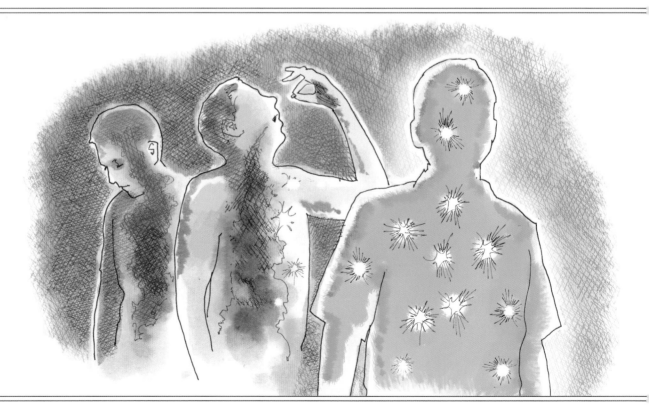

rapid mood swings and nausea set off by the smell of cigarette smoke. Sometime during the day he was separated from his friends, panicked and was overcome with anxiety. He also suffered hallucinations, specifically "hearing" colors and "seeing" sounds. This individual would have mental image pictures of everything connected to that drug incident, including imagination and the hallucinations caused by the LSD. And those pictures could unexpectedly affect him at a later time.

Sometime in the future, if this person's environment were to contain enough similarities to that past LSD incident, he could experience a reactivation of it. For example, he might be outside on a hot day and hear loud music playing. Then someone nearby might light a cigarette and blow the smoke in his direction. These factors are enough to trigger the drug-induced experiences of that day at the concert. His heart might suddenly begin racing and he might feel nauseous. He might also become overwhelmed with anxiety for no apparent reason. And then again, he might experience the same type of hallucinations involving sight and sound. In other words, without taking any more of the drug, the mental images could be restimulated and he could re-experience that drug incident.

On the other hand, there is the matter of drug residuals. Residues from the LSD he took that day at the concert remain trapped in his body. Even years later, some of those LSD crystals could suddenly become dislodged from fatty tissue and release back into his system. In so doing, the drug would be activated and send him on a new "trip," as if he had just taken more LSD.

Therefore, on the Purification Program, two factors must be considered:

1. The actual drugs and toxic residuals in the body
2. The mental image pictures of the drugs and the mental image pictures of one's experiences with these drugs

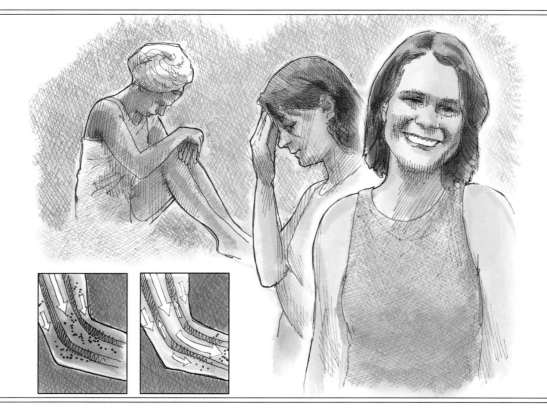

One vitamin in particular, niacin, is vital to the effectiveness of the Purification Program. Taken in sufficient quantities, niacin appears to break up and unleash residual drug and toxic residues from the body tissues and cells.

These two factors are hung up, one playing against the other, in perfect balance. What the person is feeling is the two conditions: the actual presence of the drug residuals and the mental image pictures relating to them.

The Purification Program handles one of these factors, the accumulated toxic residuals. And this fixes the person up so that the other factor, the mental image pictures, are no longer restimulative or in constant restimulation. It is as simple as that.

What happens on the Purification Program, among other things, is an upset of this perfect balance. Suddenly the balance and cross-reaction are gone. The harmful and restimulative chemical residues are flushed out and gone. This does not, however, mean the mental image pictures are gone. But they are no longer in restimulation and they are not being reinforced by the presence of drug residuals.

By breaking up the balance between these two factors and handling the toxic residuals on the Purification Program, we remove elements destructive to the individual's physical health and free him for mental and spiritual gain. In other words, the person is now in a state where he can pursue betterment of his own perceptions and abilities.

The Purification Program: A "Long-range Detoxification" Program

Even someone off drugs for years still has "blank periods." Drugs can injure a person's ability to concentrate, to work and to learn. Drug residues can stop any mental help. They also stop a person's life!

While the Purification Program originally addressed the handling of accumulated drugs in the system, it also appears to flush out many other toxic substances accumulated by the body.

As a person goes through the program and flushes out impurities, the effects of drugs, medicines and even radiation can be reactivated. These effects become less and less and eventually disappear.

These substances must be eliminated if one is to get stable mental and spiritual gain. The operating rule is that mental actions and even biophysical actions (methods of improving the person's ability to handle one's body and environment) do not work in the presence of life-hostile elements.

So, in rehabilitating an individual, only when we have accomplished a biochemical handling can we then go on to the next step, the biophysical handling (improving the person's awareness of the environment and ability to face the present) and then on to further mental and spiritual improvement.

My development of a program to handle drugs, along with drug and chemical deposits in the body, was based on the fact that successful rehabilitation of an individual can only be accomplished in the sequence outlined above. When one tries to move these steps around and put them out of sequence, one gets losses. Moreover, a full rehabilitation requires all steps to be done.

Apparent gain occurs by cleaning up the body and can be seen as an end-all in itself, though that was not the original motivation. In view of what it evidently accomplishes, however, the Purification Program might be termed a long-range detoxification program. But it should be identified as itself, since it is unique among detoxification programs, both in its procedure and reported results. To my knowledge, no other method exists by which these locked-in accumulations may be eliminated from the body.

Freed of the harmful and hindering effects of drugs and toxins, one will then be in the best possible shape to attain the lasting spiritual benefits that are available on the program. This is, of course, the sole and ultimate objective of the Purification Program.

Among other carefully researched nutritional supplements necessary for the flushing of toxic deposits is a generally misunderstood niacin, from the B complex family. As Ron explains below, his examination of the vitamin was both extensive and lengthy. Indeed, well before drug abuse became a pandemic scourge, niacin had been a definite point of study as an antidote to radiation exposure. The full story of what is referenced here regarding the testing of atomic weapons on United States military personnel surely ranks among the darkest footnotes of the twentieth century. For with full knowledge of what may follow from abnormally high radiation exposure, some two thousand marines were intentionally stationed within three miles of the largest atmospheric nuclear weapon's test ever conducted within the continental United States. The consequences, in terms of ensuing cancer clusters and related illness, were devastating—and all the more so when factoring in leukemia rates among downwind populations. As also referenced here, however, niacin proved itself an extraordinarily effective catalyst for the discharging of radiation, and continues to prove so in the wake of spillage from nuclear reactors.

The cases are startling and often miraculous, with the discharge of radiation burns in the precise pattern originally received earlier. For example, from those 2,100 marines to participate in the Nevada tests of June and July 1957 comes this initial report:

"We were told to bend down in the ditch and cover our eyes with our forearms. When that blast went off, I could see the bone in my arm through my closed eyes.... We were thrown back and forth in that ditch. It was like a stampede of cattle went over us. The force and heat were tremendous. We had burns on the back of our necks. We weren't prepared ahead of time for any of this.... We were as innocent as children until that bomb lit up the sky as bright as day and I turned to see a manikin behind me with its face on fire."

After enrollment on the Purification Program some two decades later (and following a myriad of physical complaints), a flush precisely matching those aforementioned neck burns appeared and then rapidly dissipated. Similarly, a victim of the Hiroshima bombing would tell of discharging a flush precisely matching flash-burns received through the window of her Hiroshima apartment. While more importantly, both cases further reported equally remarkable improvements as to health, clarity of thought and increased vitality.

NIACIN, THE "EDUCATED" VITAMIN

by L. Ron Hubbard

NIACIN, AS ONE OF the B complex vitamins, is essential to nutrition. It is so vital to the effectiveness of the Purification Program that it requires some extensive mention here.

The biochemical reactions of niacin are my own discovery, made in the course of research spanning three decades.

Niacin can produce some startling and, in the end, very beneficial results when taken properly as part of the program (along with the other necessary vitamins and minerals in sufficient and proportionate quantities). But its effects can be quite dramatic and so one should have a good understanding of what niacin is and does before starting the Purification Program.

In particular, niacin appears to break up and unleash LSD from the tissues and cells. It can rapidly release LSD crystals into the system and send a person who has taken LSD in the past on a trip. (One fellow who had done the earlier Sweat Program for a period of months and who believed he had no more LSD in his system took 100 mg of niacin and promptly turned on the reactivation of a full-blown LSD trip!)

Niacin has the same effect on residues of marijuana and other drugs, along with various toxic substances. Hence this vitamin is an integral component to the Purification Program. Running and sweating must be done in conjunction with taking niacin to ensure the toxic substances released by niacin do get flushed from the body.

Niacin and Radiation

Among the most startling manifestations brought about by niacin is that it can turn on, in a red flush, a sunburn on a person's body, revealing the unmistakable outline of a bathing suit.

I first encountered this phenomenon in experiments I conducted in the 1950s. Strangely, at the time, both British and American pharmacopeias (books describing drugs and their uses) advertised that this substance, niacin, turned on a flush and was therefore toxic in overdoses.

However, I discovered that if niacin was continued, in what the pharmacopeia would term "overdose," eventually one got no more flushes from it. Specifically the sunburnlike flushes would eventually disappear at a dosage of 200 mg, then at 500 mg they would recur but with less intensity. One might then get a small reaction for several days at 1,000 mg, after which one might administer 2,000 mg and find no more effects. The person would feel fine, the "sunburn" gone, and he would experience no more flush from the niacin.

But if niacin were toxic, how was it that the more one "overdosed" it, the sooner one no longer experienced the sunburnlike flushes from it?

The writers of the pharmacopeia or the biochemist may continue to think that niacin turns on a flush and that it will always turn on a flush in "overdoses." But the interesting part of it is the fact there comes a point when it *doesn't* turn on a flush. This doesn't happen by conditioning of the body; that is not what occurs.

Niacin will often cause a very hot flush and prickly, itchy skin, which can last up to an hour or longer. It may also bring on chills or make one feel tired.

It appears that niacin runs something out. In the case of the pattern of a bathing suit showing up, it is running out a sunburn, really a radiation burn. It also turns on nausea, skin irritation, hives and colitis, all of which are symptoms of radiation sickness.

Niacin, then, apparently has a catalytic effect on running out radiation exposure. So the Purification Program is not only for drugs: the quantities of niacin taken in combination with the heat of the sauna appear also to run out a certain amount of the accumulated radiation in people.

Running through Past Deficiencies

In theory, niacin apparently does not do anything by itself. It is simply interacting with niacin deficiencies that already exist in the cellular structure. For example, it does not turn on allergies; it appears to run out allergies. Evidently anything niacin does is the result of running out and running through past deficiencies.

The manifestations niacin produces can be quite amazing. Some of the somatics (physical pains and discomforts) and manifestations have already been mentioned: LSD trips, sunburns and the symptoms of radiation exposure. A person may also turn on flu symptoms, gastroenteritis, aching bones, upset stomach or even a fearful or terrified condition. In fact, there seems to be no limit to the variety of phenomena that may occur with niacin. If it is there to be run out by niacin, it apparently will do so with niacin.

The two vital facts proven by observation are these:

1. When the niacin was carried on until these things discharged, they did then vanish, as they *will* do.

    It is a matter of record that a reaction turned on by niacin will turn off where administration of niacin is continued.

"In particular, niacin appears to break up and unleash LSD from the tissues and cells. It can rapidly release LSD crystals into the system and send a person who has taken LSD in the past on a trip."

2. When the niacin dosage was increased and the whole lot of the rest of the vitamins being taken was also increased proportionately, the niacin itself, taken in large amounts, did not create a vitamin deficiency.

On the Purification Program, therefore, the progressive increase of the niacin dosages determines the proportionate increase of the other vitamins and minerals. And in fact, it is niacin that monitors completion of the Purification, for when one no longer feels the effects of past drugs and toxins, one has achieved the product of the program itself.

Niacin's biochemical reaction was a pivotal discovery, one that made an incalculable contribution to the successful results of the Purification Program.

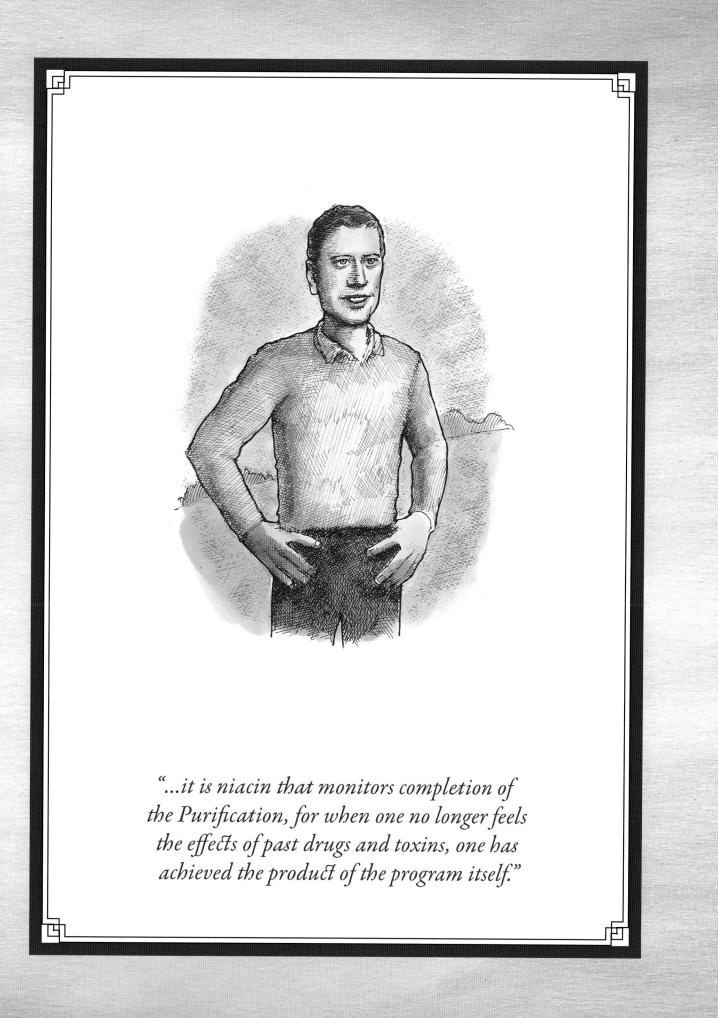

"...it is niacin that monitors completion of
the Purification, for when one no longer feels
the effects of past drugs and toxins, one has
achieved the product of the program itself."

Scientific and Professional Appreciation

With inevitable talk of L. Ron Hubbard's purification and detoxification methods within medical/scientific circles came the inevitable scientific appreciation. In the main, laboratory and clinical interest focused on two aspects of the LRH discovery. First, of course, the environmental physician had not generally suspected toxic residues were stored in the body; while those who may have suspected never imagined fatty tissues to be the culprit. In either case, no effective means of flushing toxins from the body was even dreamed possible; hence the emphasis on prevention, rather than treatment. In the end, however, one cannot argue with results. Presented here is but a small sampling of statements from those who measure efficacy with meticulous care.

Anna C. Law, MD
Gerald T. Lionelli, MS
Ambulance Industry Journal, May/June 1989
Vol. 9 No. 3

"The Hubbard method has become the only method of human detoxification in broad clinical use. Reports published by the Royal Swedish Academy of Sciences, the World Health Organization's International Agency for Research on Cancer and others have shown it to be a safe and effective method of reducing body levels of common environmental contaminants and alleviating the symptoms associated with exposure to them."

James G. Dahlgren, MD
Assistant Clinical Professor of Medicine, UCLA

"I have devoted the last thirty years to research, health screening and other activities related to the health effects of toxic exposures. I have evaluated the health status of hundreds of firefighters in cities throughout the country.

"The exposures resulting from the WTC disaster are unprecedented. The toxic dust, fume and vapor that arose from the collapsing World Trade Center and subsequent fire contained hundreds of different toxic chemicals including dioxins, PCBs, asbestos, silica, benzene, polybrominated diphenyl ethers, manganese, chromium, lead, mercury, nickel, oxides of nitrogen and sulfur.

"This is a very short list of the toxics that were present. The combustion products from the fire created a host of toxic substances that have not been well characterized, but are known to be important factors in fire toxicology.

"In addition, the force generated by the collapse of the towers was so great that it created ultrafine particles of these toxins—smaller than have ever been seen before. The 'dust' that

"I've now put nearly 4,000 individuals through
the Hubbard Detoxification Program.
I can say without a doubt
that it works."

was created was in many ways more like a gas, rendering the body mechanisms intended to protect the lungs useless.

"It is not surprising, therefore, that serious respiratory problems have resulted from the WTC exposures. But these symptoms are only the first that can be anticipated....

"For example, it is likely that firemen diagnosed as having 'Post-traumatic Stress Syndrome' are in fact suffering from neurological injury caused by the numerous neurotoxins that were present at the event.

"The Hubbard Detoxification Program is the only method that exists that offers the possibility of reducing the body burdens of toxics that can cause disease. Let me repeat that: it is the only method that has shown promise in this regard."

David E. Root, MD, MPH
Senior Medical Advisor
New York Rescue Workers
Detoxification Project

"I've now put nearly 4,000 individuals through the Hubbard Detoxification Program. I can say without a doubt that it works. It's still the only treatment that addresses the effects of accumulated toxins. And there's nothing else on the horizon."

The commemorative fireman's helmet bestowed in recognition to what the Purification Program represented to Emergency Rescue personnel suffering from toxic exposure in the wake of 9/11. The inscription reads: *"To our brother, L. Ron Hubbard, from your brothers at the New York City Fire Department, we honor you with this helmet, a symbol of our motto, 'To Protect Life and Property' which the legacy of your technology embodies."*

CHAPTER THREE

Drugs, the Mind and
THE HUMAN SPIRIT

Drugs, the Mind and
the Human Spirit

" MY RESEARCH FOR MANY, MANY YEARS HAS BEEN CARRIED out with the purpose of freeing Man spiritually. My original inquiry was into the nature of Man and the bulk of my work has always addressed Man as a spiritual being. When barriers to this arose, those barriers merited further research and resolution." —L. Ron Hubbard

The statement is enormously significant and bears upon the whole thrust of L. Ron Hubbard drug rehabilitation methods. That is, the problem of substance abuse is finally a problem of the human spirit and cannot be resolved unless addressed accordingly. Thus L. Ron Hubbard drew from central principles of Dianetics and Scientology to clear a path for a spiritual ascent. That his terrain involved such matters as perceptual experience, emotions and sensations in no way means the solution is intangible. On the contrary, it is every bit as tangible as a four-hundred-dollar-a-day habit. That a materialistically grounded medical community has so enthusiastically embraced his procedures is likewise beside the point. The fact remains that all we are about to examine follows from a spiritual equation.

(While conversely, the impetus for modern usage is bound up in a materialistic equation wherein everything we think and feel is held to be a chemical recombination within the brain. Thus the implicit pharmaceutical argument: if our lives are imperfect, then let's mess with the chemistry.)

The fundamentals are these: When speaking of resolving the *mental* and *spiritual* aspect of drug use, one is speaking of employing the central practice of Dianetics and Scientology, which is processing or auditing (from *audire*, to listen). It is delivered by an auditor, who employs an Electropsychometer, or E-Meter, to measure one's mental state or change of state and so help pinpoint otherwise unseen sources of personal travail. Neither evaluative nor ambiguous, processing has nothing to do

While the Purification Program rids the body of drug residues, complete freedom from drugs and the damaging consequences requires that one address mental image pictures associated with drug use. This processing, known as the Drug Rundown, handles the mental and spiritual repercussions of usage and is delivered by highly trained practitioners in Scientology churches and missions.

One originally turns to drugs for a reason—some physical suffering or hopelessness. The problem is thus essentially spiritual. The user was suffering and drugs became the solution for unwanted feelings or conditions.

with psychology or psychotherapy. Rather, it is the means of better understanding oneself through precisely worded processes, allowing one to discover one's own basic truths. The whole is predicated upon the fact we are potentially all-knowing and beneficent spiritual beings and if only we might understand the source of our troubles, then we shall be troubled no more.

When speaking of rehabilitating the drug user through processing within Dianetics and Scientology, one is speaking of those processes collectively known as the *Drug Rundown*. It addresses not only the deeper consequences of usage, but also those factors precipitating usage in the first place. It is exclusively delivered by highly trained practitioners within the Church of Scientology, and if a truly comprehensive appreciation of the procedure requires a fairly thorough grasp of Scientology principles, the essentials are simple enough.

PAIN

TANGLED
MENTAL IMAGE
PICTURES

PAST INCIDENT

{ *Perceptions and mental recordings of experience while on drugs are
inaccurate, to say the least—a combination of memory, imagination
and the actual event of the time. Consequently the user's memory
of past experience is tangled up with present time experience.* }

Drug use, even medicinal or recreational usage, tends to foster a severe disassociation from reality. (Witness the severely unreal vein that characterized psychedelic art.) The user is also routinely out of communication or out of touch, and otherwise all but dysfunctional. Then, too, and with some emphasis, Ron speaks of the user as not wholly "tracking" with the real-time events and not perceiving what others perceive. For having sought escape from a seemingly unbearable present, he finds himself

fixed in an illusory past. The matter is acute; it explains the very real parallels between usage and insanity, and so becomes the first point of address through the Drug Rundown. That is, through what is termed *objective processing,* the former user is reoriented to the present and relieved of obsessive fixation on drug-related experience.

Beyond objective processing come procedures for addressing the actual impact of drugs on the mind. In particular, and quite in

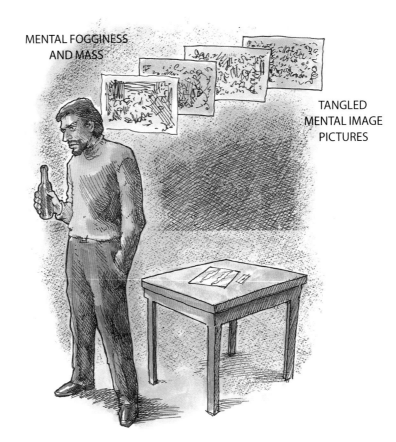

MENTAL FOGGINESS AND MASS

TANGLED MENTAL IMAGE PICTURES

{ *In essence, then, the mental pictures are scrambled in his mind to one degree or another. Thus, his memory and his ability to think are both seriously impaired.* }

addition to what drugs wreak in purely physical terms, users retain a consecutive record of

"...one must appreciate the user was invariably troubled prior to usage or would never have turned to drugs in the first place."

all drug experience in the form of mental image pictures. These pictures are literally three-dimensional recordings of perceptual experience, including emotions, speculations and conclusions. Although frequently beyond volitional control, the recording of the drug experience contains actual energy or mental *charge,* which may exert considerable influence upon intellectual capacity, behavior and bodily functions. Moreover—and this is unique to the drug case—the user retains mental image pictures of hallucinatory experience—some

Precise procedure that has the individual address the experiences that he had while he was taking drugs

Discovering and examining the source of drug-related sensations

PAIN

PAIN

The Drug Rundown, then, handles the mental and spiritual aspect of usage. It first addresses experiences while taking drugs with precise procedures, alleviating fixations from those experiences. By discovering and examining the source of these sensations, the harmful mental energy is discharged.

of it quite gruesome and impacting upon thinking in ways that are both insidious and horrifying.

Addressing the drug experience, relieving attendant trauma and restimulation from drug-related memory—this, then, becomes the next step of the Drug Rundown. In purely technical terms, the Drug Rundown becomes the process of identifying accumulated mental charge from drug experience, inspecting that charge and exhausting it. Also addressed are drug-related attitudes, emotions, sensations and pains—all likewise components of mental image pictures and capable of reactivation even decades after usage. Hence the former user's all-too-common complaints of psychosomatic ailments, perceptual impairment, emotional shut-off and failing cognitive skills. Hence too, why many a former user will speak of a time when he felt himself brighter, healthier, more capable and alive.

Precise procedure that has the individual address the underlying impetus for usage and the unpleasant physical, emotional and mental sensations linked to it

PAIN

EMOTION

Discovering and examining what was wrong before drugs became the solution or "cure"

{ *Finally, the Drug Rundown addresses the underlying impetus for usage and the unpleasant physical, emotional and mental sensations linked to it. In other words, the final step of the rundown addresses what was wrong before drugs became the solution or "cure." If the underlying cause of usage is not resolved, the need or compulsion remains.* }

As regards the final aspect of the Drug Rundown—the resolution of those factors precipitating usage—one must appreciate the user was invariably troubled *prior* to usage or would never have turned to drugs in the first place. That trouble may have been physical, emotional or any of the myriad of difficulties so commonly ascribed to the inadequacies of modern existence. But regardless, the problem of drug use is *always* preceded by a problem of living. Moreover, that problem must be

resolved before one is actually free from the *need* and, frankly, it is only resolved through the Drug Rundown.

Given the Drug Rundown is a wholly subjective process and predicated upon the fact that one must ultimately discover his own answers, it may be quite impossible to appreciate the revelation here without the experience. Nevertheless, let us appreciate this much: although conventional theory holds the addict to be permanently scarred—that

The Drug Rundown, therefore, resolves unwanted feelings both during *and* prior to the usage of drugs, alcohol or medicine. It is a solution in the truest sense of the word; for the actual compulsion is removed. A full resolution, then, of drug use requires *all* these steps.

{ *The freer one's attention from the past, the more able he is to deal with life. In short, he feels brighter, enjoys increased perception, increased control of himself and surroundings, and better interacts with others.* }

his craving may be suppressed or replaced but never conquered, the damage from addiction never repaired—the Drug Rundown proves otherwise, and categorically so. Indeed, all we have seen in the way of results from the Purification Program and the Narconon program represents but a fraction of potential gains from the Drug Rundown. As a matter of fact, those completing the rundown routinely report increased vitality, abilities and intelligence *over and above* predrug levels.

Presenting another statement on what it means to spiritually rehabilitate those who fall prey to drug abuse is L. Ron Hubbard's "The Road Out." That his tone is measured, even understated, is appropriate. That message is a simple statement of fact. For given Scientology indeed provides a sure road back from hard-core addiction, what else can one possibly say? ■

With the employment of Dianetics and Scientology principles for the rehabilitation of incarcerated addicts comes the oft-quoted LRH letter to all concerned. Those familiar with Ron's extensive work for the moral and ethical salvation of criminals will recognize the voice: firm but sincere, understanding but not didactic and, above all, honest. Those familiar with the larger story of Dianetics and Scientology will recognize sentiment: here are discoveries "by the people and for the people," as he so famously phrased it and those discoveries are intended for use by anyone.

THE ROAD OUT

by L. RON HUBBARD

THERE ARE TWO WAYS to escape the raw deal that this universe sometimes hands out.

One is to go to sleep or wholly unreal and forget it.

The other is to attain a calm, serene beingness that is proof against the knocks and arrows of misfortune.

The first method has distinct liabilities. However, it is the most usual route taken by human beings who find the going too rough.

Alcohol, drugs, self-hypnotism are all men have been prone to use.

The only real trouble with them is that one wakes up into the same world, but a bit weaker, a bit redder of eye, feeling a bit worse.

The drug or other knocks on the head didn't change the universe any and one is still in it, still catching it, probably with an even lower resistance to it. So the first method is not a very good one.

The second method, the ability to rise above it all, has long been preached. But unfortunately there wasn't any readily available technology to accomplish it.

In the way back areas of Tibet, in the Lama Monasteries, one was supposed to be able to find technology with which, if one practiced it for twenty years, one could rise above suffering and become a serene being.

But tickets to Tibet didn't grow on trees and, besides, the country has been gobbled up by an overpopulated China.

It's one thing to hear that one should rise above it all and quite another to do it.

In the early 1930s, while in Engineering School, I found that Man didn't have an adequate mental technology. In the East, before that, I had heard of mental abilities not known in the West. But they had the liability that they took too long and were somewhat like the old story about turning lead to gold. If you went up on a hill in the full of the Moon and put a lead block on a phosphorescent tree stump and said "Abracadabra," the lead would turn to gold, *providing* you did not think of the word "Hippopotamus"!

So anyway, I saw that Man didn't really have a mental technology, didn't really have a real road out.

Off and on up to World War II, I worked on the problem and made some progress. But after the war, when I saw so many of my friends overwhelmed and beaten by life, I stepped up the speed of advance and by 1950 had developed and released Dianetics.

"In the 1968–69 year of research, I was finally able to map an easy road which could be traveled despite drugs, despite the starting point. And of course that made it easier for everybody."

Two years later, research had entered the field of the human spirit, the soul, the life unit we call a *thetan,* and Scientology was born.

With the additional developments of nineteen years since the first release of Dianetics, the road out is definitely there, definitely established and a few hundred thousand, at a conservative estimate, have taken it and benefited from it.

Well, you know all that. But just this year a further breakthrough occurred.

In 1968 the percentage of cases coming into orgs who had been on drugs rose to at least 40 percent.

The road out is the road of increased awareness. It is not a wholly painless road.

Those who had already taken the road down had a rough time going up again.

If they increased their awareness enough, they would arrive at a high level where they were at cause and in which they could not only cope with their environment, but could prosper in it, well above the reach of suffering.

But how to get them *up* from the point to which they had already gone down?

In the 1968–69 year of research, I was finally able to map an easy road which could be traveled despite drugs, despite the starting point. And of course that made it easier for everybody.

Drugs do odd things to the mind. This makes it a bit rough to begin to go up.

The breakthrough was Dianetics again. By using Dianetics to prepare the way for Scientology, most ill effects of drugs could be erased, the reasons one began on them could be handled and then the upper tech of Scientology worked very fast.

To give you some idea of the magnitude of the breakthrough, in 1950 some cases went two thousand hours on Dianetics. In the 1969 development, fifty hours is a high number to a superior result. Also, in 1950 it took months to make a Dianetic Auditor. In the developments of 1969, this has been reduced to two and a half weeks of full-time study for a bright fellow and not more than three months of part-time study for a rather slow student. The new STANDARD Dianetics, as it is called, handles all cases.

Standard Dianetics uses an E-Meter and a standard text and is taught in a very standard way.

It is interesting that the 1950 book, *Dianetics: The Modern Science of Mental Health,* now issued as a paperback edition for newsstands, has again all by itself surged up once more to the bestseller list. It was this book which the head of all US prisons ordered all his wardens to read in 1950.

Standard Dianetics is a full professional subject which has been realigned to make it invariably useful when exactly taught and used.

It would be relatively easy to procure the full course, to study the HDG Study Pack first, to get some meters and turn out Standard Dianetic Auditors with minimal help from the outside.

This would put any determined group well up there on the road out and would certainly eradicate the past effects of drugs and make one a well and happy human being.

Scientology would then be fully and broadly effective and results, a lot higher than they ever achieved in Tibet, would be easy.

I would feel pretty bad if a lot of good guys had to live with the road blocked. And I don't see any real reason why Standard Dianetics so taught wouldn't be fully effective.

Like anybody else, I have had my own share of slings and arrows over the years and I know what it is like.

It isn't all that easy to help one's fellows and to be helped in return. But the end product is itself worth a lot of slings and arrows.

The road out is the way up.

I hope you make it.

Best of luck.

Ron

Narconon Arrowhead on Lake Eufaula, Oklahoma: international training center for the L. Ron Hubbard rehab program

CHAPTER FOUR

NARCONON

Narconon

EXCLUSIVELY UTILIZING L. RON HUBBARD'S DRUG rehabilitation technology is the worldwide network of Narconon centers. An acronym for *narcotics—none,* Narconon began in 1966 when an Arizona State Prison inmate named William Benitez happened on a basic Scientology text by L. Ron Hubbard.

Employing principles therein to kick an eighteen-year heroin habit, Benitez organized a pilot course with twenty fellow inmates likewise nursing habits. Shortly thereafter, he enlisted LRH permission and support to found a formal Narconon program. Upon his release in 1967 (delayed by choice to complete implementation of the program), Benitez founded a first residential center in California. Thereafter, with continued support from L. Ron Hubbard in particular and Scientologists in general, Narconon became what it is today: the singularly most effective and extensive drug rehabilitation network on Earth.

In a word, Narconon employs the full battery of L. Ron Hubbard technologies for withdrawal and rehabilitation. The lineup includes assists, objective processes and communication drills, combined with recommended nutritional supplements for a "First Step" withdrawal that is swift and relatively painless. With the student then capable of real-time functioning, detoxification begins through the Narconon New Life Detoxification Program. Largely free from physical craving, the student is next enrolled on life improvement courses. In sum, these courses provide all requisite skills/tools with

Left Another view of Narconon Arrowhead: the facility further provides training and on-site internships for rehab professionals from more than a dozen nations

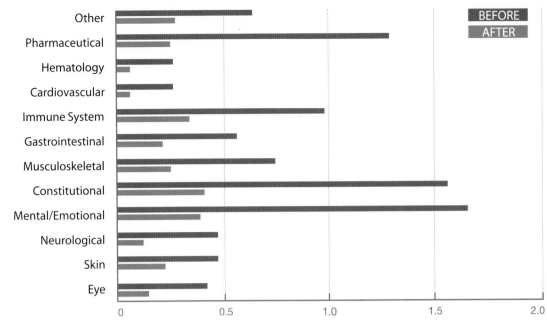

SYMPTOM SEVERITY IN DRUG USERS

BEFORE
AFTER

Other
Pharmaceutical
Hematology
Cardiovascular
Immune System
Gastrointestinal
Musculoskeletal
Constitutional
Mental/Emotional
Neurological
Skin
Eye

0   0.5   1.0   1.5   2.0

Above
Studies show the considerable reduction of toxic symptoms after L. Ron Hubbard's Purification Program

which he may successfully make his way in life—succeeding where he has failed, setting and achieving worthwhile goals where he previously had none. Included in the lineup is a Personal Values & Integrity Course wherein the student both assumes responsibility for past transgressions and regains a sense of self-worth (yet another crucial factor in the cycle of addiction). Also included is an Ups & Downs in Life Course to identify and resist those who might encourage reversion. (That addiction is invariably linked to the criminal/anti-social associations is the failing of many less-comprehensive programs; thus the Narconon graduate is thoroughly proofed against those who would lead him back to usage.)

Further included is L. Ron Hubbard's common sense moral code and guide to living, *The Way to Happiness*. Appealing to people of all faiths and persuasions, the booklet is a potent force against drug abuse and criminality across two hundred nations. In point of fact, *The Way to Happiness* played no insignificant role in quelling narcopolitical violence in Colombia.

It is the Narconon program in total, however, that generates the talk within rehabilitation circles. The Commission on Accreditation of Rehabilitation Facilities (CARF) is the United States independent accrediting organization. It is recognized by government entities and insurance carriers alike, and so determines acceptable standards of care for the field. It is not for nothing, then, that a CARF evaluation of Narconon found the program quite unparalleled. That is, when Narconon is viewed vis-à-vis the greater rehabilitation field: "In terms of outcome...it is far above."

Equivalent European studies concluded the same. In a notoriously drug-ridden Spain (principal pipeline for European trafficking), nonrecidivism rates of 20 percent are exemplary. Hence the astonishment when independent Spanish evaluations found close to 80 percent of those graduating Narconon remained wholly drug-free. Swedish studies proved equally unparalleled—and particularly against general rehabilitation success rates averaging but 15 percent and frequently as low as 1.6 percent. In highly dramatic contrast, then, follow-up

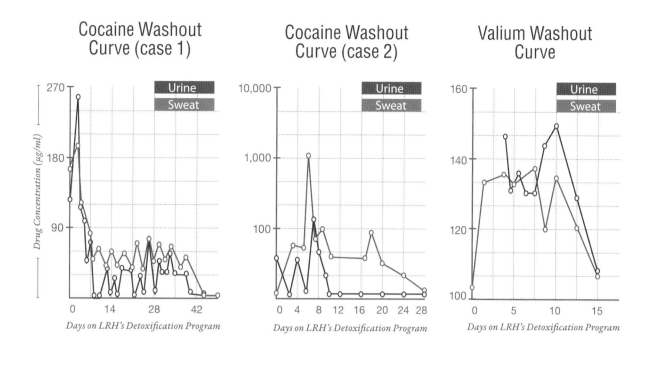

Cocaine Washout Curve (case 1)

Drug Concentration (μg/ml)

270

180

90

Urine
Sweat

0   14   28   42

Days on LRH's Detoxification Program

Cocaine Washout Curve (case 2)

10,000

1,000

100

Urine
Sweat

0 4 8 12 16 20 24 28

Days on LRH's Detoxification Program

Valium Washout Curve

160

140

120

100

Urine
Sweat

0   5   10   15

Days on LRH's Detoxification Program

studies found 78.6 percent of those emerging from Narconon Sweden were still drug-free after four years—which is to say, that for all intents and purposes, these people were cured.

One could cite significantly more: outcome studies of a Narconon program aimed at juvenile offenders found nearly 90 percent of those completing the program remained felony-free. Narconon has further earned a singular reputation for curing the so-called intractable addict no other private facility will touch. But however one assesses Narconon success, the point is not difficult to appreciate. "This program deserves the attention of the addiction community," writes the Rehabilitation Accreditation Commission's leading surveyor, "and I would recommend that other professionals investigate this unique program."

To exactly that end—providing the Narconon program to others across the rehab

field—stands the Narconon Arrowhead training center at Lake Eufaula in Oklahoma. It is the world's largest residential drug rehabilitation and training center, and affords rehab professionals with both theory and practice of the Narconon program. That Arrowhead's international academy further admits the nonprofessional underscores another crucial fact about the Narconon program—that unparalleled Narconon success rate is not dependent on some undefined "knack" gained through years of trial and error. Rather, success follows from L. Ron Hubbard's codification of a rehabilitative regimen addressing all key mental and physiological components of drug addiction. Moreover, that regimen can be swiftly learned, easily implemented and delivered to addicts in a variety of settings—from free-standing residential and nonresidential centers to community and correctional facilities.

Left
L. Ron Hubbard's rehabilitative regimen of life-skill courses keep former users from ever again reverting to drugs

In dramatic emphasis of the latter, the late 1990s saw a graduate of the Narconon international training center initiate the program within one of Mexico's most notorious prisons. It was a place where inmate heroin consumption ran better than 90 percent and featured a sanctioned "shooting gallery" adjacent to the main latrine, where prisoners were all but invited to inject. Violence was also endemic, for what with a population described as only technically alive, no one had much to lose. Yet at the literal center of that institution, Narconon established a pilot withdrawal, detox and rehab facility—replete with sauna and course rooms. Immediately beyond the first phase, all participants were drug-free and surrounding cellblock heroin consumption dropped an estimated 80 percent.

Results were similarly dramatic in a Utah juvenile center implementing Narconon methods for drug-offense probationers. It was administered by probation officers themselves. It immediately enjoyed success beyond anything imagined possible and in the words of a presiding juvenile court judge: "From my vantage point it is incredible to see the transformation that occurs over a period of time in the faces of the youth and their parents."

EFFECTIVENESS OF NARCONON

80%

15%

Average Success Rate

Narconon Success Rate

20% is considered exemplary

Description of Narconon Courses

Drug-free Withdrawal. The first step of the Narconon program. Helps the individual rapidly cease current drug use with minimal discomfort through an L. Ron Hubbard regimen of assists, objective processes, proper nutrition and care from experienced Narconon staff.

Narconon's Learning How to Learn Course. Provides students with L. Ron Hubbard's acclaimed learning and literacy tools for dramatically increased comprehension and retention of knowledge. Armed with these tools, students can proceed to further educational steps toward productive and ethical lives.

Narconon's The Basics of Communication Course. Employs drills developed by L. Ron Hubbard to extrovert students, enabling them to comfortably face life and resolve problems through communication.

Narconon's Purification & Detoxification. Cleanses the body of drug residues and other toxic substances through a regimen of exercise, sauna and nutritional supplements. This step effectively purges drug residues that rekindle cravings and wreak emotional havoc.

Narconon's Perception & Orientation Course. Brings students into communication with others and environment. Extroverts students from disturbing memories associated with drug use and releases fixated attention, allowing students to view the world around them, often for the first time in years.

Narconon's Overcoming Ups & Downs Course. Provides students with the ability to spot and handle those in their environment who would otherwise cause them to lose gains and resume drug use. In short, students gain new stability in the face of destructive influences and learn to wisely choose friends and associates.

Narconon's Personal Values & Integrity Course. Utilizes yet another body of L. Ron Hubbard tools. Students gain an invaluable insight into personal ethics, honesty and integrity. They learn what it means to assume responsibility for transgressions, thus freeing themselves from ill effects of past misdeeds.

They further gain an ability to immediately correct non-survival behavior.

Narconon's The Conditions of Existence Course. Teaches students to apply L. Ron Hubbard's step-by-step procedures for improving upon all activities, endeavors and relationships. With this technology, students are able to reassert their self-determinism and chart a survival course in life.

Narconon's The Way to Happiness Course. Based on L. Ron Hubbard's common sense, nonsectarian moral code, *The Way to Happiness.* This course provides students with a guide to living wherein real happiness is attainable and conduct translates into greater survival for all. ∎

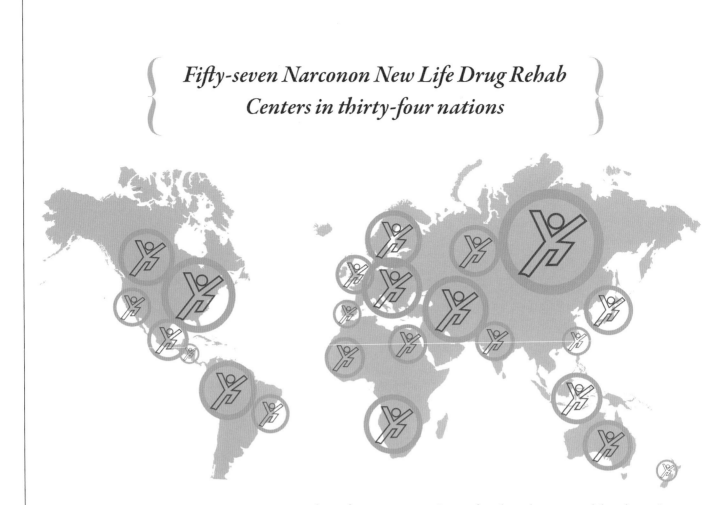

In consequence, courts increasingly refer addicts to Narconon in lieu of jailtime.

There is more again farther afield. Narconon Nepal was originally founded by a veteran police officer grown weary of arresting addicts.

exist. It's artificial and is caused by drugs." It is also inherently unproductive, anti-social and can precipitate acts of extreme violence. Consequently, it is not for nothing that long-standing substance-abuse counselors

"...the problem of substance abuse is finally a problem of the human spirit and cannot be resolved unless addressed accordingly."

Graduations are attended by heads of Nepalese state and a locally famed mountain was renamed in L. Ron Hubbard's honor as "Hubbard's Peak." Narconon Nepal is additionally renowned for drug prevention through education. It is another Narconon specialty—presenting the unabashed "truth about drugs" through lectures to at-risk youth. Accordingly, the Narconon Nepal team addresses Katmandu schools en masse—in fact millions of children to date—with consequent drops in drug-related crime to all-time lows.

But to reiterate L. Ron Hubbard's critical observation: "The drug personality does

tell of participating in Narconon programs wherein graduates exhibited such a pronounced change "that I sometimes think I have made a mistake and am not sitting opposite a former heroin addict." Then, too, so pronounced is the physical change—the clarity of eyes, improved skin tone—parents frequently speak of scarcely recognizing previously addicted sons and daughters. Then again, there is all that follows from succeeding steps of the Narconon program and is probably best expressed by the Narconon graduates themselves: "I am not only reacquainted with life, but reacquainted with myself."

DEALT IN DRUGS

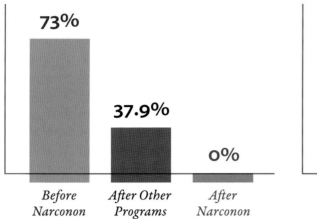

73%

37.9%

0%

*Before
Narconon*

*After Other
Programs*

*After
Narconon*

COMMITTED ROBBERIES

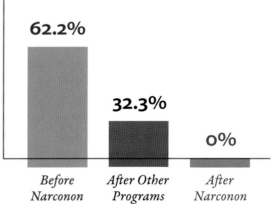

62.2%

32.3%

0%

*Before
Narconon*

*After Other
Programs*

*After
Narconon*

What such statements finally represent to a pandemic drug crisis is, frankly, only dependent on how swiftly and broadly L. Ron Hubbard's rehabilitation methods are utilized. For however else one weighs the evidence here, the fact remains that half of those entering Narconon previously sought treatment in any number of state and private clinics. Some were temporarily successful. Others, supplying psychiatric replacement drugs, only compounded the problem. But either way, those stepping drug-free from Narconon will typically describe L. Ron Hubbard as the greatest friend they have ever known. And should you challenge the statement, they will ask in turn: *Have you any conception of how it feels to be free from a twenty-year habit?* ◼

Republic of the Philippines
Office of the President
DANGEROUS DRUGS BOARD
This

PLAQUE OF RECOGNITION
is awarded to

L. RON HUBBARD

as a symbol of our gratitude for his humanitarian work in the field of
drug education and drug rehabilitation and for his relevant technologies
which are adopted and implemented in the Philippines through
the various programs, projects and activities of the Church of
Scientology, the Foundation for a Drug-Free Philippines,
the Drug-Free Ambassadors Australia, the Narconon International,
and the Volunteer Ministers, thus contributing immeasurably to the
successful pursuit of our noble vision of a drug-free country.
Ang lahat na ito ay nagpapatunay ng kanyang pagmamahal
sa Pilipinas at sa buong daigdig.

Given this 13th day of March, 2008 at the DDB Conference Room,
Quezon City.

SEC. ANSELMO S. AVENIDO, JR.
Chairman, DDB

A few of the many thousands of accolades afforded
L. Ron Hubbard in recognition of his drug rehab technology

Epilogue

"We live in a chemical-oriented society," wrote L. Ron Hubbard, and the problem is only compounding. For having accepted drug consumption under a banner of emotional and behavioral control, we are very much out of control. And make no mistake, those consuming psychotropic drugs are no less part of the problem than addicts strung out on illicit drugs. Merely, with multibillion-dollar pharmaceutical campaigns aimed at increasingly larger population bases, prescription drug use is so pervasive it is all but a way of life...a slow way of death.

So let us not lose sight of the answers presented herein. Because unless we come to grips with what drugs have wrought, this society will indeed combust in a biochemical conflagration. Then, too, let us not forget that when discussing L. Ron Hubbard's solution, one is discussing something far closer to the heart of the problem than stricter enforcement, tighter regulations and tougher warning labels. Rather, and very simply: One is offering a person his life.

"You may have noticed that society is rapidly going downhill. Inflation, lack of fuel and even war cast deep shadows over the world. And the most serious part of this is that drugs, both medical and street drugs, have disabled a majority of those who could have handled it, including the political leaders, and have even paralyzed the coming generations."

APPENDIX

GLOSSARY

A

abound: occur or exist in great quantities or numbers. Page 34.

abundance: a large quantity that is more than enough. Page 34.

acceleration: increase in how fast something happens. Page 36.

acclaimed: praised publicly with great enthusiasm. Page 1.

accolades: awards, honors or expressions of high praise or great regard for someone. Page 84.

accreditation: the action of officially recognizing a person or organization as having met a standard or criterion. Page 76.

accustomed to: used to; in the habit of. Page 37.

acid: another term for *LSD*. *See also* **LSD.** Page 11.

Acid Dreams: a 1986 account of the history of LSD, including the CIA's use of it in mind-control experiments, by American authors Martin A. Lee and Bruce Shlain. Page 11.

acquitted: cleared of a charge, as by being declared not guilty. Page 30.

addiction: the condition of taking harmful drugs and being unable to stop taking them. Page 1.

additive(s): substances added directly to food during processing, as for preservation or to change its texture or color. Page 29.

adverse(ly): creating results that are harmful. Page 30.

afford: supply or provide something. Page 28.

agent: 1. something, such as a chemical substance, organism or the like, that causes an effect. Page 1.
2. a means by which something is done or caused. Page 20.

Agent Orange: the military code name for a powerful chemical substance that destroys plants and weeds, used by the United States armed forces during the 1960s and early 1970s in the Vietnam

War. Named for the orange stripe on its containers, Agent Orange was used to strip trees and plants of their leaves and kill crops in the jungles and farms of South Vietnam and the Southeast Asian country of Laos. This served to reveal enemy hiding places and destroy their sources of food. Agent Orange contained the highly poisonous substance dioxin. Various health problems afflicting American and other servicemen in Vietnam are thought to have resulted from exposure to the dioxin in Agent Orange. Page 28.

aggravated: characterized by some feature defined by law that increases the severity of a crime, such as the intention of the criminal or the special vulnerability of the victim. Page 30.

agricultural: of or having to do with *agriculture,* the occupation, business or science of cultivating the land, producing crops and raising animals for food. Page 34.

airline travel miles: a reference to any of the programs offered by airline companies that allow people to receive credit (designated as miles, kilometers, points or the like) when they travel on the airline, use a certain credit card, stay at certain hotels or fulfill certain other requirements. These credits can then be redeemed for free air travel or for other goods and services. Page 2.

all but: almost; very nearly. Page 9.

allergy(ies): a condition whereby a person has an unusual sensitivity to a normally harmless substance that, when breathed in, ingested or brought into contact with the skin, provokes a strong reaction from the person's body. Page 52.

alleviate: lighten or lessen the pain, severity, etc., of something; relieve. Page 5.

all too: quite; altogether. Used to emphasize that something is the case to an extreme or unwelcome extent. Page 36.

Alpert, Richard: an early experimenter with hallucinogenic drugs who, from his position as a Harvard University professor of psychology, spread the myth of the benefits of drugs. In later visits to India, he became involved in Eastern philosophy, changing his name to Ram Dass and authoring books on mysticism. Page 12.

ambiguous: open to or having several possible meanings or interpretations. Page 61.

"amnesia beams": a form of radiation with high frequencies in the same range as microwaves (a form of nonvisible energy used in radar, radio transmissions, cooking or heating devices). Researchers have shown that exposure to such radiation has been capable of bringing about memory loss. Page 11.

amounted to: totaled; added up to. Page 13.

amphetamine: any of a group of powerful, habit-forming drugs, called *stimulants,* that act on the central nervous system (the brain and the spinal cord), increasing heart rate and blood pressure while reducing fatigue. Exhaustion and depression follow when the effects of the amphetamine wear off. Serious mental problems can develop from repeated use. Page 1.

antidepressant(s): the name given to a class of drugs prescribed by psychiatrists and physicians as a solution for "depression" and expanded to include a wide range of symptoms, from decreased appetite to fatigue. Antidepressants deaden one's emotions and often bring about a highly agitated state. Some of the side effects include not only dizziness, fainting, severe headaches, raised blood pressure, difficulty sleeping and interference with sexual function, but also homicidal and suicidal thoughts and behavior. Page 2.

antidote: something that prevents or counteracts harmful or unwanted effects. Page 10.

anti-nerve gas: a substance intended to counteract the effects of *nerve gas,* any of several poisonous chemicals that can be inhaled or absorbed through the skin, causing paralysis, especially of the respiratory system, and leading to death. Anti-nerve-gas substances have been shown to be harmful to the body when several of them are used together, a practice that was common during military operations in the Persian Gulf. Page 28.

anxiety: feelings of worry, nervousness or concern, especially about something that is about to happen. Page 30.

Apollo: from the late 1960s through the mid-1970s, the upper-management activities for all Churches of Scientology over the world were conducted from a fleet of ships, the main vessel being the *Apollo.* The 350-foot (110-meter) vessel also served as L. Ron Hubbard's home and center for his many research activities. Page 14.

apparent: readily perceived or understood; obvious. Page 41.

apparently: according to what seems to be the case, as supported by evidence. Page 3.

array: a large group, number or quantity (of things). Page 9.

arsenic: a silvery-white, brittle, very poisonous chemical element. It is used in a wide range of products from glass and lead to military poison gases and insecticides. It is most commonly lethal in large doses, but repeated inhalation of the gases or dust can also be fatal because these accumulate in the body. Page 35.

asbestos: a mineral that was used in building construction until it was discovered to be a cause of certain cancers. Asbestos has been used for insulation and fireproofing because of its heat-resistant properties. Page 38.

aspect: one side or part (of something); a phase or part (of a whole). Page 4.

assault rifle: a military automatic rifle that can be fed by a large-capacity magazine (a chamber for holding a supply of cartridges to be fed into a gun automatically). The term *assault* is used to refer to a weapon designed for use in warfare, especially when used in noncombat situations. Page 31.

assist(s): a process that can be done to alleviate a present time discomfort and help a person recover more rapidly from an injury or illness. (A *process* is a set of questions asked, or commands given, by a Scientology or Dianetics auditor to help a person find out things about himself or life and to improve his condition.) Page 75.

at large: as a whole; in general; (taken) altogether. Page 35.

atmospheric nuclear weapon's test: the testing of nuclear bombs by exploding them in the atmosphere. Approximately one hundred such tests were conducted at the Nevada Test Site during the 1950s and early 1960s, with another eight hundred tests conducted underground from the 1960s until the early 1990s. The largest atmospheric bomb test, part of a series of twenty-four tests that occurred between May and October 1957, occurred in early July 1957, when a bomb of more than 70 kilotons was exploded. (A *kiloton* is a measure of force of the explosive capability of a nuclear weapon. One kiloton is equivalent to the explosion of a thousand tons of *TNT,* a powerful chemical explosive.) *See also* **blast; downwind; Nevada.** Page 50.

atmospheric poison: any poison that exists in a particular atmosphere. An example of atmospheric poison would be a toxic chemical ejected into the air of a town from a factory, poisoning the atmosphere for all those in the town. Page 33.

atomic: having to do with atomic energy, which is produced when the central part of an atom (nucleus) splits apart. The pieces of the nucleus then strike other nuclei (centers of atoms) and cause them to split, thus creating a chain reaction accompanied by a significant release of energy. Atomic bombs, as used in an atomic war, produce atomic energy. There is another type of atomic energy found in power plants. Although the energy is used for good purposes, it can be highly dangerous to those working in the plants if a leak occurs. One example of an atomic power plant explosion is Chernobyl in the Ukraine, in 1986, wherein an atomic generator exploded and sent radioactive debris 0.6 miles (1 kilometer) into the air, where wind carried radioactive dust to as far away as Sweden. Page 40.

atrophy: shrinking or weakening of some organ or body part, usually caused by injury, disease or lack of use. Page 36.

attendant (to): accompanying or connected with or following as a result of. Page 3.

auditing: the application of Dianetics and Scientology techniques (called *processes*). Processes are directly concerned with increasing the ability of the individual to survive, with increasing his sanity or ability to reason, his physical ability and his general enjoyment of life. Also called *processing.* Page 61.

auditor: a Dianetics or Scientology practitioner. The word *auditor* means one who listens; a listener. Page 61.

autopsy(ies): the medical examination of a dead body to establish the cause and circumstances of death. Page 44.

axiomatic: self-evident; obviously true. Page 20.

B

banner: a guiding principle, cause or philosophy, from the literal meaning of *banner,* a flag on a pole, such as one used in battle by a country or a king. Page 10.

barbiturates: drugs used in medicine to calm people or make them sleep. Page 11.

battery: any large group or series of related things. Page 75.

B complex: a group of vitamins found in yeast, cereal, nuts, eggs, liver and some vegetables. B complex includes vitamins B_1, B_2, niacin (vitamin B_3), B_6, B_{12} and others and helps in breaking down carbohydrates. Page 50.

bear out: prove something to be true; confirm. Page 39.

bears upon: relates to or affects something. Page 20.

behavioral: having to do with the way in which an individual acts or conducts himself or herself. Page 9.

being: a person; an identity. Page 20.

benchmark: pertaining to or used as a standard of excellence, achievement, etc., against which anything similar must be measured or judged. Page 1.

beneficent: doing acts of goodness or kindness. Page 62.

beneficial: improving a situation; helpful, useful or favorable. Page 51.

benzene: a toxic liquid derived from petroleum, having a distinctive odor and used in the manufacture of dyes and industrial chemicals. Inhaling benzene vapor is harmful to the body. It can damage the bone marrow that forms blood cells, leading to leukemia. Page 56.

bestowed: given or presented as a gift. Page 57.

biochemical: the interaction of life forms and chemical substances. *Bio-* means life; of living things. From the Greek *bios,* life or way of life. *Chemical* means of or having to do with *chemicals,* substances, simple or complex, that are the building blocks of matter. Page 1.

biochemist: one who is trained in and who practices *biochemistry. See also* **biochemistry.** Page 52.

biochemistry: the chemical properties, reactions and phenomena of living matter. Page 44.

biophysical: of or relating to the application of methods of improving a person's ability to handle his body and environment. Page 49.

black art: a technique or practice that is mysterious and sinister. Literally, another term for *black magic,* a form of magic attempted for evil purposes, as by calling upon evil spirits or the devil. Page 9.

Black Death: the name given to a form of *bubonic plague,* a highly contagious and often fatal disease that spread over Europe and much of Asia in the fourteenth century, killing more than fifty million people, roughly a quarter of the population. Page 20.

blast: an explosion of a bomb; also the accompanying *blast wave,* the highly compressed air that is like a wall moving rapidly away from the *fireball,* the cloud of dust and extremely hot gases created when the bomb explodes. Violent winds and intense radiation and heat accompany the blast. *See also* **Nevada.** Page 50.

Bluebird, Chatter, Artichoke: a series of mind-control programs running in the United States from 1947 through 1953. Chatter (1947–1953) was a United States Navy program focusing on the identification and testing of drugs in interrogations and the recruitment of agents. Bluebird was a CIA mind-control program established in 1950, dealing with interrogation, behavior modification and related topics. It was renamed Artichoke in 1951 and in 1953 was replaced by MKULTRA. *See also* **MKULTRA.** Page 10.

bluntly: in a manner that is direct and straightforward. Page 35.

body burden(s): the amount of a specific toxin, or the total amount of toxins, that have built up in a person's body over a period of time. Page 57.

bolstered: given support or aid, in order to continue on; strengthened or encouraged, often in an illegal or immoral activity. Page 15.

B₁: a vitamin found in green peas, beans, egg yolks, liver and the outer coating of cereal grains. It assists in the absorption of carbohydrates and enables carbohydrates to release the energy required for cellular function. A *carbohydrate* is one of the three main classes of food (the others are fats and protein) that provide energy to the body. Page 37.

borne out: proven to be true; confirmed. Page 44.

Bowart, Walter: Walter Howard Bowart (1939–2007), author of the book *Operation Mind Control,* an investigative report published in 1978 that detailed government mind control through the use of drugs such as LSD, behavior modification, hypnosis and the like. Page 11.

boy soldier: a reference to the practice in some parts of Africa and Asia of drafting preteenaged boys as soldiers. Page 4.

Brave New World: the title of a satirical novel (1932) by British author Aldous Huxley (1894–1963), describing a supposed futuristic utopia (an ideal state) that is tightly regimented by the government; uses science to control reproduction, intelligence and behavior; and employs drugs to keep the populace calm and agreeable. The society is strictly divided into classes, each with its own appointed intelligence, function and codes of behavior. *Brave* here means fine or splendid. Page 20.

break (broken) down: make a substance separate into parts or change into another form in a chemical process. Page 42.

breakdown: a collapse or failure. Page 3.

bringing to light: revealing or making known. Page 38.

bucket, drop in the: a small, usually inadequate, amount in relation to what is needed. Page 2.

building block: literally, a large block of concrete or similar hard material used for building houses and other large structures. Hence anything thought of as a basic unit of construction, such as an element or component regarded as contributing to something's growth or development. Page 33.

bulletin: a reference to a *Professional Auditor's Bulletin,* one of a series of issues written by L. Ron Hubbard between 10 May 1953 and 15 May 1959. The bulletins carried the newest technical advances in Dianetics and Scientology, reprints of the latest procedures and technical issues released. Page 11.

BZ: a code name for a chemical weapon manufactured from *benzilic acid,* a chemical related to benzene. When BZ is inhaled, it produces incapacitating physical and mental effects. Page 13.

C

cancer: a serious disease in which cells in a person's body increase rapidly in an uncontrolled way, producing abnormal growths. Page 39.

cancer cluster: the occurrence of a greater-than-expected number of cancer cases within a group of people in a geographic area over a period of time. Atmospheric testing of nuclear bombs at the Nevada Test Site during the 1950s and early 1960s created fallout that has resulted in a higher incidence of certain cancers in the ensuing years. *See also* **fallout** and **Nevada.** Page 50.

candid: truthful and straightforward; frank. Page 31.

cap it: apply the finishing touch to something; complete something. Page 4.

cardiovascular: relating to both the heart and the blood vessels. Page 76.

case(s): 1. any individuals or matters requiring or undergoing official or formal observation, study, investigation, etc. Page 9.

2. a general term for a person being treated or helped. It is also used to mean the entire accumulation of upsets, pain, failures, etc., residing in a person's mind. Page 17.

3. an instance of something; an occurrence; an example. Page 21.

catalyst: a substance that increases the rate of a chemical reaction without itself undergoing any change. Page 50.

catalytic: involving or causing an increase in the rate of a chemical reaction by the use of a *catalyst. See also* **catalyst.** Page 52.

catching it: getting into trouble or getting punished. Page 69.

categorically: absolutely, certainly and unconditionally, with no room for doubt, question or contradiction. Page 67.

cellular: relating to or consisting of living cells (the smallest structural unit of an organism). Every second of the day, millions of cells in the human body die and are replaced by new cells as an essential part of the normal cycle of cellular activity. Page 34.

cerebral cortex: the outer gray matter of the brain associated with functions such as voluntary movement, coordination of sensory information, learning and memory. Page 15.

charge: harmful mental energy accumulated in the mind, which can affect a person, as with feelings of anger, fear, grief, apathy or the like. Page 64.

chemical warfare: military operations involving poisonous gases and chemicals as weapons. Page 35.

chilling: causing a feeling of dread or horror. Page 15.

chills: unnaturally lowered body temperature accompanied by shivering. Page 52.

chromium: a hard metallic element used to increase hardness and resistance to corrosion in other metals. Certain types of chromium compounds are toxic to the lungs and can cause lung cancer. Page 56.

CIA: the Central Intelligence Agency, a United States Government agency created in 1947. The stated purpose of the CIA is to gather information (intelligence) and conduct secret operations to protect the country's national security. Page 10.

circulation: the movement of blood around the body. Page 42.

cite(d): mention, especially as an example of what one is saying. Page 2.

clean up: eradicate harmful influences or elements (from within something). Page 49.

clinical: 1. purely scientific. Also, based on actual observation of individuals rather than theory. Page 3.
2. of, relating to or connected with a clinic (a facility devoted to the diagnosis and care of patients who receive treatment without staying overnight). Page 56.

coal tar: a thick, black, sticky liquid produced in the processing of coal. Coal tar compounds are used in making dyes, drugs, explosives, food flavorings, perfumes, etc. Page 39.

cocaine: a powerful and highly addictive stimulant drug that acts on the central nervous system (the brain and the spinal cord), increasing heart rate and blood pressure while reducing fatigue. Because cocaine can cause dangerous side effects and addiction, many countries have made it illegal. Page 1.

codeine: a drug obtained from opium, used as a painkiller or sedative and to inhibit coughing. (*Opium* is an addictive drug prepared from the juice of the poppy plant.) Page 44.

code name: a name used to disguise the identity or nature of something—for example, a military operation. Page 10.

cognitive: of or pertaining to the mental processes of perception, memory, judgment and reasoning. Page 65.

colitis: inflammation of the colon, characterized by diarrhea, fever, lower-bowel spasms and upper-abdominal cramps. Page 52.

colloquially: in a manner that is informal or characteristic of or appropriate to ordinary or familiar conversation rather than formal speech or writing. Page 28.

Colorado: a state in the western United States. Page 31.

combust: figuratively, be consumed as if by fire. Page 87.

coming generations: the next or future *generations,* entire groups of individuals born about the same period. Page 87.

commemorative: intended as something that honors and keeps alive the memory of a great person. Page 57.

commensurate(ly): (in a manner) that corresponds in size or degree to something else; proportionately. Page 4.

commonplace: encountered often. Page 34.

composite: made up of several parts or elements. Page 14.

compound: 1. a substance composed of two or more parts in exact proportions. Page 10.

2. increase or intensify. Page 41.

comprehensive: including everything, so as to be complete. Page 46.

concentration camp, Nazi: a reference to the practice of conducting medical experiments on prisoners in Nazi Germany concentration camps during World War II (1939–1945). *Concentration camps* were a type of prison camp established for the confinement and persecution of Jews, political opponents, religious dissenters, etc. In such camps, along with the mass extermination of prisoners, thousands of persons were subjected to inhuman and highly abusive "medical" experiments. *See also* **Nazi.** Page 10.

conditioning: causing to become accustomed to something, making someone or something adapt (to a particular situation, treatment, environment, etc.). Page 11.

conflagration: something that, like a huge, disastrous fire, consumes everything. Page 87.

Congressional inquiries: investigations initiated by Congress (the supreme lawmaking body of the United States) to look into governmental affairs, executive actions or public and private wrongdoing. Congressional inquiries may lead to new laws. Such investigations, carried out by Congress as a body or by appointed committees, have been launched to uncover scandals and to spotlight certain issues where reform is needed. Page 10.

conjunction with, in: together with. *Conjunction* means an instance of coming together. Page 51.

constitutional: of or relating to a person's physical or mental state. Page 76.

consumption: the action of taking something (such as a drug, food or liquid) into the body by swallowing, inhaling or absorbing it. Page 1.

coolant: a substance used to reduce the temperature of a system by conducting away the heat produced in the operation of the system. Coolants used in industry, also called *heat transfer fluids,* are found particularly in electrical equipment and also in cooling the edges of tools that cut metal. Page 28.

correlative: having a mutual or complementary relationship. Page 27.

cosmopolitan: containing or having experience of people and things from many parts of the world. Page 14.

count: a reference to a measurement of radiation as measured on a Geiger counter (an instrument that is used for detecting and measuring radioactivity). If something has a high count, it is highly radioactive. Page 40.

counterculture: of or concerning a culture with values and mores that run opposite (counter) to those of established society. Page 12.

course of, in the: during the progress or length of. Page 36.

cross-reaction: a (sometimes negative) response that comes from both sides of something. *Cross* in this sense means involving a mutual interchange. Page 48.

crystal(s): small, irregular solid formations of material, used here specifically referring to small deposits of LSD (or any similar drug) stored in the tissues of the body. Page 47.

cumulative: increasing in effect, size, quantity, etc., by successive additions. Page 40.

cyclical: of or pertaining to a cycle or cycles, or characterized by recurrence in cycles. A *cycle* is a period of time during which a characteristic, a regularly repeated event or a sequence of events occurs. Page 28.

D

Dade County, Florida: a county at the southern tip of *Florida,* a state in the southeastern United States that is a peninsula lying between the Atlantic Ocean and the Gulf of Mexico. The county, also called Miami–Dade County, is also the metropolitan area of its principal city, Miami, which is a major seaport and resort. Page 30.

deal, raw: harsh or unfair treatment. Page 69.

debilitated: weakened or reduced in strength or energy. Page 36.

decrying: expressing strong disapproval of or openly criticizing somebody or something; condemning openly. Page 5.

deduced: came to a conclusion by reasoning from known facts. Page 27.

deduction(s): a conclusion drawn from available information. Page 30.

defeatist mechanism: a means of causing people to surrender easily or no longer resist defeat because of the conviction that further effort is futile (incapable of producing any result). Page 34.

defoliant: a chemical sprayed or dusted on trees and plants that causes their leaves to fall off, sometimes used in warfare to deny cover to enemy forces. Page 28.

deposit(s): an accumulation of material in a body tissue, structure or fluid. Page 27.

depressant: also called *sedative,* a drug or agent that has the effect of slowing the rate of the body's muscular or nervous activity. Page 9.

de rigueur: strictly required, as by current usage. Page 20.

derivative: a substance obtained from, or regarded as having come from, another substance. Page 39.

detoxification: the action of removing a poison or a poisonous effect from something, such as from one's body. Page 27.

devastating: causing enormous shock, upset or destruction. Page 13.

Dianetics: Dianetics is a forerunner and substudy of Scientology. Dianetics means "through the mind" or "through the soul" (from Greek *dia,* through, and *nous,* mind or soul). It is a system of coordinated axioms which resolve problems concerning human behavior and psychosomatic illnesses. It combines a workable technique and a thoroughly validated method for increasing sanity, by erasing unwanted sensations and unpleasant emotions. Page 1.

didactic: overly instructive, characteristic of one who teaches rigid rules and principles. Page 68.

diet: 1. used to describe a food or drink that is intended for people trying to lose weight, usually because it is low in calories or fat or contains a sugar substitute. Page 39.

2. the food that a person eats and drinks regularly. Page 45.

dioxin: a highly toxic chemical that occurs in some pesticides and defoliants (chemicals that remove leaves from trees), known to cause cancer and birth defects. Page 28.

disarrange: unsettle or disturb the order or proper arrangement of; throw out of order. Page 44.

disassociation: the state or condition wherein things connected to or similar to each other are not seen to be related or are seen to be different, or things that have no relation are conceived to be related or similar. Page 15.

discharge: go away so as to be free or rid of (something). Page 50.

discriminate: involving a choice; not random. Page 3.

dislodge: force or knock something out of its position. Page 43.

dispelled: caused to be removed. Page 43.

distorted: changed in shape or appearance so that (something) is not clear or in the correct order. Page 46.

distraught: extremely upset and distressed. Page 9.

do in: attack or kill (someone). Page 37.

doled out: given out in equal portions or according to a prescribed allotment; distributed. Page 3.

dominant: more important, powerful or noticeable (than other things). Page 41.

Doors of Perception, The: a 1954 book written by British author Aldous Huxley (1894–1963) detailing his experiences when taking the hallucinogenic drug mescaline. The title of the book is based on a passage from *The Marriage of Heaven and Hell,* a work by English poet, artist and mystic William Blake (1757–1827): "If the doors of perception were cleansed every thing would appear to man as it is, infinite. For man has closed himself up, till he sees all things through narrow chinks of his cavern." Page 12.

dosage(s): an amount of something, usually a vitamin, medicine or drug, that is taken regularly over a particular period of time. Page 27.

downwind: in a position further along the line of the direction of the wind, used here in reference to the general pattern of winds that blow from southern Nevada across parts of adjoining states, including Utah, Arizona and New Mexico. During the 1950s and early 1960s, when atmospheric testing of nuclear bombs was occurring at the Nevada Test Site, radioactive fallout from the explosions was blown across and into these areas, resulting in a higher incidence of certain cancers in the ensuing years. *See also* **atmospheric nuclear weapon's test.** Page 50.

dramatic: great, marked or strong, etc. Page 27.

Dr. Jekyll and Mr. Hyde: a reference to the novel *The Strange Case of Dr. Jekyll and Mr. Hyde,* written in 1886 by Scottish author Robert Louis Stevenson (1850–1894). In this story Dr. Jekyll is a kindly, well-liked physician who develops an interest in the dualism of personality. Experimenting with drugs, he succeeds in separating the good and evil sides of his own nature, the latter being intermittently personified as Mr. Hyde. He eventually cannot control his transformations and, as the evil Mr. Hyde, he commits a murder. To eliminate this evil character, Dr. Jekyll commits suicide. The phrase *Jekyll and Hyde* is used figuratively to describe a person who alternates between two extremely different personalities, usually one charming and good, the other evil and repulsive. Page 4.

drop in the bucket: a small, usually inadequate, amount in relation to what is needed. Page 2.

Drug Enforcement Agency: an agency of the United States Government, established in 1973 through a merger of four separate drug-law-enforcement agencies and charged with the responsibility to enforce laws concerning narcotics and other dangerous drugs. Page 3.

druggies: drug addicts. Page 36.

Drug Rundown: done after the Purification Program, this rundown unburdens the effects of a person's drug use. By addressing the mental and spiritual damage that results from drug use, one experiences considerable relief and expansion as a spiritual being. The result is a person released from the mental and spiritual effects of drugs, medicine and alcohol. *See also* **rundown.** Page 41.

drum: a large cylindrical container used for storing liquids, for example, oil or chemicals. Page 39.

drying out: of a drug addict or alcoholic, undergoing a course of treatment designed to break dependence on a drug or alcohol. Page 17.

dynasty: a sequence of rulers of the same family or group. Page 18.

dysfunctional: unable to deal adequately with normal social relations. Page 63.

E

educated: as if in possession of intellectual powers. Page 51.

efficacy: capability of producing a desired result or effect; effectiveness. Page 56.

electroshocked: subjected to *electroshock,* the firing of 180 to 460 volts of electricity through the brain from temple to temple or from the front to the back of one side of the head. It causes a severe convulsion (uncontrollable shaking of the body) or seizure (unconsciousness and inability to control movements of the body) of long duration. Page 9.

element: one of the factors playing a part in or determining the outcome of some process or activity. Page 5.

Eli Lilly: an American pharmaceutical company that develops and manufactures medical and psychiatric drugs. Page 12.

eliminated: removed or gotten rid of. Page 42.

elimination, processes of: procedures for the removal of something. Used here in reference to the usual routes (such as the pores of the skin) by which a body gets rid of unwanted particles from within it. Page 43.

Elizabeth, New Jersey: a city in northeastern New Jersey, USA, which was the location of the first Hubbard Dianetic Research Foundation, 1950–1951. Page 9.

embedded: firmly or deeply fixed in a surrounding mass. Page 44.

embody: give a tangible or visible form to (an idea or quality) through words, actions, etc. Page 57.

E-Meter: full name *Electropsychometer,* from electro (electricity), psyche (soul) and meter (measure); an electronic device for measuring the mental state or change of state of Homo sapiens. It is not a lie detector. It does not diagnose or cure anything. It is used by auditors to assist a person in locating areas of spiritual distress or travail. Page 61.

encampment: a group of tents or temporary shelters put in one place; camp. Page 4.

end-all in itself: a purpose or goal desired for its own sake (rather than to attain something else). Page 49.

endemic: characteristic of a specific group of people. Page 78.

"enhancer(s)": something designed to improve, but which actually reduces, the quality of something. Page 39.

enlisted: gained the cooperation or support of. Page 12.

espionage: the use of spies by a government or organization to discover the military, political or technical secrets of other nations or organizations. Page 11.

essential: necessary; important in a particular situation or for a particular activity. Page 40.

essentially: basically or fundamentally, used when referring to the true or basic nature of something. Page 34.

ethical: of or having to do with agreed principles of correct moral conduct. Page 36.

ethics: rationality toward the highest level of survival for self and others. Page 81.

Eufaula, Lake: a lake in the eastern part of Oklahoma, a state in the south central part of the United States. Page 72.

euphemistic: said of a mild, indirect or vague expression substituted for one thought to be offensive, harsh or blunt. Page 30.

evidently: clearly. Used to indicate that something is undoubtedly true because it is there to be seen. Page 18.

evolved: worked out or developed, especially by experience, experimentation or intensive care or effort. Page 43.

excessive: more than is usual; going beyond a usual or normal limit or degree. Page 40.

excess of, in: more than. Page 2.

exemplary: serving as a model or example. Page 76.

exhausting: figuratively, removing something completely, as if from an area or region where it has been contained. Page 65.

expose: 1. make (a crime, etc.) known; reveal wrongdoings, especially by publishing or broadcasting the information. Page 10.

2. cause someone to experience or be at risk of. Page 28.

exposition: a setting forth of facts, ideas, etc.; detailed explanation. Page 4.

exposure: the experience of coming into contact with something, such as an environmental condition, that has a harmful effect. Page 28.

extensive: 1. having a wide scope; far-reaching or thorough. Page 10.

2. great in amount or number. Page 40.

extract: a substance that has been taken out of a compound by using an industrial or chemical process. Page 39.

exudation: the giving off or oozing out (of moisture), in the manner of sweat through the pores. Page 43.

F

factoring in: including as an essential element. Page 50.

faddism: a fondness for fads or a tendency to follow fads. A *fad* is a temporary fashion, idea, manner of conduct, etc., that is embraced with great enthusiasm and that is usually short-lived. Page 34.

fallout: airborne radioactive dust and material shot into the atmosphere by a nuclear explosion, which then settles to the ground. Page 40.

fat(s): one of the three main classes of food (the others are proteins and carbohydrates) that provide energy to the body. Fats provide a highly concentrated source of energy for the cells; serve as building blocks for the membranes that surround every cell in the body; and help blood to clot and the body to absorb certain vitamins. Fats occur in foods derived from both animals and vegetables. Page 42.

fatty tissue: a kind of body tissue containing stored fat that serves as a source of energy; it also cushions and insulates vital organs. Page 4.

felonious: constituting a *felony,* a serious crime, typically one involving violence. Page 13.

fiber: an essential character or quality. Page 36.

First Cavalry Airmobile: the US Army division that used helicopters during the Vietnam War to attack targets and transport troops. Page 13.

fission: the splitting (fissioning) of the nucleus (center) of an atom into fragments, accompanied by a tremendous release of energy. Page 40.

five bucks a hit: the amount paid (five dollars) for a *hit,* a quantity of a narcotic drug used at one time. Page 15.

fixation: an instance of being *fixated,* having the attention commanded exclusively or repeatedly (on something); obsessive preoccupation. Page 63.

flagship: the best or most important one of a group or system. Page 78.

Flaming Youth era: the time period of the 1920s, when young people in America adopted a lifestyle characterized by vigorous and unrestrained behavior or ways. Young women cut their hair short and wore short skirts. The favorite haunts were nightclubs where young people drank illegal liquor (Prohibition was in force from 1920 to 1933), listened to jazz (the latest musical craze) and danced. Page 18.

flashback: a memory, past incident or event occurring again vividly in one's mind. Specifically, with certain drugs (such as LSD and similar drugs), it is the reemergence of some aspect of the hallucination (which took place while on the drug) in the absence of the drug. The most common form includes altered visual images; wavering, altered borders to visual images; or trails of light. Page 15.

Florida: a state in the southeastern United States, lying mostly on a peninsula between the Atlantic Ocean and the Gulf of Mexico. Page 28.

flower children: young persons in the 1960s and 1970s who rejected conventional society and advocated love, peace and simple, idealistic values. The term *flower child* came from their custom of wearing or carrying flowers as a symbol of peace. Page 13.

flush: a red color that appears on the face or body, sometimes when hot, or the hot feeling itself within the body. Page 50.

flush (out): get rid of harmful substances in a part of the body or the whole body by using a large amount of liquid. Page 27.

footnotes: extra comments or information added to what has just been said. Page 50.

free-standing: not affiliated with others of its kind; independent. Page 77.

full-blown: possessing all the qualities or features to be fully or completely developed. Page 15.

fully: entirely or wholly; to the full extent of the time, quantity or number specified. Page 22.

furtive: characterized by guilty or evasive secrecy; stealthy. Page 2.

G

gain: an improvement or resurgence; any betterment of the individual. Page 29.

gastroenteritis: inflammation of the stomach and intestines, causing vomiting and diarrhea. *Gastro* means stomach. *Entero* means intestines and *-itis* means inflammation or swelling. Page 52.

gastrointestinal: relating to the stomach and intestines. Page 76.

generations, coming: the next or future *generations,* entire groups of individuals born about the same period. Page 87.

Georgia: a state in the southeastern United States, on the Atlantic Ocean. Page 31.

gobbled up: taken; seized or grabbed as if by *gobbling,* swallowing or eating hastily or hungrily in large pieces. Page 69.

gradiently: gradually approaching something; taking something step by step, level by level. Page 45.

grain(s): the smallest unit of weight in the system of weights used in the United States, Great Britain and Canada, originally based on the weight of a single grain of wheat. A grain weighs 1/7,000 pounds and is equal to approximately 0.065 grams. Page 35.

Grateful Dead: an American rock band that started in the mid-1960s, often performing in the Haight-Ashbury district of San Francisco (the center for the hippie and drug culture at that time) and playing what was known as "psychedelic music." Page 12.

grips with, come to: begin to understand and deal with directly or firmly. *Grip* means the grasping of something tightly and in this sense refers to a mental or intellectual hold on something. Page 28.

Ground Zero: the site of the World Trade Center attacks on 11 September 2001. Originally a term referring to that part of the ground situated immediately under an exploding nuclear weapon. Page 28.

Gulf War: also *Persian Gulf War,* a war between Iraq and a number of countries organized mainly by the United States and the United Nations (UN). It occurred in 1991, prompted by Iraq's invasion of the tiny oil-rich nation of Kuwait, both countries situated at the northern end of the Persian Gulf. Page 28.

Gulf War Syndrome: a collective group of medical ailments reported by veterans who served in the Persian Gulf War (1991). The term *Gulf War Syndrome* or *Illness* emerged in the years following the war, when up to 100,000 of the 697,000 United States troops who had served in the Persian Gulf came to Veterans Affairs Medical Centers with complaints of mysterious ailments they attributed to their wartime service. *See also* **Gulf War.** Page 28.

H

Haight-Ashbury: a neighborhood in San Francisco, California. During the 1960s Haight-Ashbury became a center for the hippie movement, also known for widespread use of drugs. Page 13.

hailed: praised or approved with enthusiasm. Page 4.

hallucination: the perception of objects with no reality and the experiencing of sensations without any external cause; the apparent perception (usually by sight or hearing) of an external object when no such object is actually present. The condition is brought about by drugs or severe illness. Page 47.

hallucinogenic: characteristic of *hallucinogens,* a type of natural or synthetic drug that produces marked distortion of the senses and hallucinations. Hallucinogens are also known to lead to anti-social thoughts, disorientation and confusion and generally produce the symptoms of severe insanity. *See also* **hallucination.** Page 12.

hand, to: easily available. Page 27.

happened on: discovered or encountered something or somebody by chance. Page 75.

harboring: keeping (a thought or feeling) secretly in one's mind. Page 3.

hardcore: characterized or regarded as fixed, unchanging or the like. Page 67.

hard put, be: have considerable difficulty or trouble. Page 33.

havoc: wide and general damage or destruction. Page 27.

HDG: the *Hubbard Dianetic Graduate Course,* a course that trained a person to teach Standard Dianetics. Page 71.

headline: given prominent notice, as in newspapers or news broadcasts. Page 12.

heavy: (of a person) using or consuming something a great deal. Page 38.

heels of, on the: closely following; just after. Page 20.

hematology: the study of the blood, blood-producing tissues and diseases of the blood. Page 76.

herbicide: a chemical preparation designed to kill plants. Page 28.

heroin: a compound derived from morphine (a drug used in medicine to relieve pain) that is illegally used as a powerful and addictive drug causing a lessened sensation of pain, slowed breathing and depression. Withdrawal symptoms include cramplike pains in the limbs, sweating, anxiety, chills, severe muscle and bone aches, fever and more. If overdosed, it can be fatal. Page 13.

high priest: figuratively, a person in a high position of power or influence; the chief supporter of a doctrine or practice. From the priest in some ancient religions who ranked above all other priests as head of the priesthood. Page 12.

Hiroshima: a seaport in Japan that was largely destroyed in 1945 during World War II (1939–1945) by an American atomic bomb. This was the first atomic bomb ever used in warfare and killed approximately 75,000 people. Page 50.

hives: a skin rash that is marked by itching and small pale or red swellings and often lasts for a few days. Page 52.

hodgepodge: a confused mixture; mess. Page 20.

hold true: be, or continue to be, true; prove true or applicable over time. *Hold* is used here to mean maintain (a condition, situation, course of action, etc.) over time. Page 36.

horizon, on the: likely to happen or exist soon, as if becoming visible. From the literal meaning of *horizon,* the furthest that one can see, where the sky seems to meet the land or the sea. Page 57.

host: a very large number; a great quantity. Page 43.

hostilities: unfriendly or aggressive feelings or behavior. Page 3.

hung up: halted or snagged. Page 48.

Huxley, Aldous: (1894–1963) British author of novels, poetry and essays. He is best known for *Brave New World* (1932), a novel foretelling a futuristic, dehumanized society in which people rely on mood-enhancing pills for relief and escape from reality. In *The Doors of Perception* (1954)

Huxley wrote of his experiences with hallucinogenic drugs. *See also* **Brave New World** and **Doors of Perception, The.** Page 12.

hypnotics: drugs or other agents that cause sleep or drowsiness. Page 4.

I

illicit: not allowed by the law; not approved of by the normal rules of a society. Page 2.

ills: problems, difficulties or things considered harmful. Page 37.

illusory: unreal; of the nature of an *illusion,* a perception that represents what is perceived in a way different from the way it is in reality. Page 63.

immune system: *immune* means relating to a body's resistance to disease or the creation of resistance. The *immune system* is the interacting combination of all the body's ways of recognizing cells, tissues, objects and organisms that are not part of itself and initiating the immune response to fight them. Page 76.

impair: weaken or damage; lessen the quality, strength or effectiveness of; make or cause to become worse. Page 64.

impede: interfere with the movement, progress or development of something. Page 34.

impetus: driving force or motive; impulse. Page 61.

implication: a likely consequence. Page 18.

implicit: implied, rather than stated directly. Page 61.

impurities: substances that are added to something else so that it is no longer pure. Impurities in the body can include drugs and other toxic chemical substances—for example, food preservatives, insecticides, pesticides, as well as any residual crystals of drugs (if the person has ever taken LSD or any similar drug). Page 48.

inaccessible: not able to be talked to; not approachable. Page 9.

incalculable: too great to be measured. Page 54.

incarcerated: imprisoned or confined. Page 68.

incident(s): an experience, simple or complex, related by the same subject, location or people, understood to take place in a short and finite time period such as minutes or hours or days. Page 42.

in-depth: very thorough and detailed. Page 46.

indicator: a sign or symptom that gives evidence of or shows (something). Page 44.

indiscriminate: done without thought about what the result may be, especially when it causes people to be harmed. Page 29.

induced: brought about, produced or caused. Page 4.

industrial: relating to or involving companies that manufacture or sell a particular product or range of products that are made from raw materials, as opposed to products that are grown and then sold. Page 28.

inflation: a higher volume of money in circulation than there are goods, resulting in a continuing rise in the general price level. Inflation gets that way because of nondelivery. Page 87.

ingest: take something (such as food, a liquid or a gas) into the body by swallowing, inhaling or absorbing it. Page 39.

ingestion: the action of taking something (such as food, a liquid or a gas) into the body by swallowing, inhaling or absorbing it. Page 4.

in lieu of: in place of; instead of. Page 82.

in light of: taking into consideration what is known, or what has just been said or found out. Page 2.

inner-city: in or of the usually older, poorer and more densely populated central section of a city, particularly when associated with social problems such as inadequate housing and high levels of crime and unemployment. Page 2.

inordinately: to an extreme degree. Page 9.

in short: introducing a summary statement of what has been previously stated in a few words; in summary. Page 35.

insidious: operating or proceeding in an inconspicuous or seemingly harmless way but actually with grave effect. Page 14.

insupportable: that cannot be *supported,* endured or borne; unbearable. Page 21.

intake: an amount taken in (by the body) or the act of taking something into the body, usually by swallowing or inhaling something. Page 33.

integral: being an essential part of something; necessary to the completeness of the whole. Page 51.

integrity: the quality of being honest and doing what one knows is right despite any urgings to do otherwise. Page 76.

interaction: the action or influence of persons or things on each other. Page 33.

interfere with (something): prevent (something) from happening as planned or as part of its usual course of action. Page 33.

International Agency for Research on Cancer: a part of the World Health Organization that attempts to identify causes of cancer so that preventive measures may be adopted against them. Page 56.

interplay with: act on; exert an influence upon; affect. Page 27.

in the course of: during the progress or length of. Page 36.

intractable: affected by a condition that is hard to treat, relieve or cure. Page 77.

intrinsic(ally): belonging to something as one of the basic and essential elements that make it what it is. Page 20.

in view of (something): because of (something). Used to introduce the reason for a decision, action or situation. Page 49.

irregulars: soldiers who are not part of an official military body. Page 13.

J

Jack the Ripper: the name given to the unidentified murderer of at least seven London prostitutes in 1888. Page 31.

Jones, Candy: professional name of Jessica Wilcox (1925–1990), one of the most successful American fashion models of the 1940s, whose photos were favored by US troops during World War II (1939–1945). Mind-control experiments involving Candy, published in the 1980s, presented her as an early victim of attempts to program individuals without their awareness by using drugs, hypnotism and the like. Page 10.

K

Katmandu: a city in and the capital of Nepal, located in the central part of the country. Page 82.

Kennedy, Robert: Robert Francis Kennedy (1925–1968), United States political leader and legislator, brother of President John F. Kennedy (1917–1963). Robert Kennedy held the positions of Attorney General (1961–1964) and senator from New York State (1965–1968). As a presidential candidate in 1968, he was shot and killed by Jordanian immigrant Sirhan Bishara Sirhan. Page 10.

Kesey, Ken: (1935–2001) American writer, author of the 1962 novel *One Flew Over the Cuckoo's Nest*. Page 12.

kick: 1. a strong but temporary interest or activity. Page 34.

2. succeed in giving up (a habit or addiction). Page 75.

knocks and arrows: a variation of *slings and arrows,* figuratively meaning calamity or misfortune, opposition, assault, etc. A reference to a passage from Shakespeare's tragedy *Hamlet,* in which Prince Hamlet of Denmark seeks to avenge the murder of his father. In one part of the play, Hamlet considers suicide:

> *"To be, or not to be: that is the question:*
> *Whether 'tis nobler in the mind to suffer*
> *The slings and arrows of outrageous fortune,*
> *Or to take arms against a sea of troubles,*
> *And by opposing end them?"* Page 69.

L

lama: a Lamaist monk. *Lamaism* is a form of Buddhism practiced in Tibet and Mongolia. *See also* **Tibet.** Page 69.

landmark: marking a significant change or turning point in something. From *landmark,* an event, idea or item that represents a significant or historic development. Page 1.

large, at: as a whole; in general; (taken) altogether. Page 35.

later-generation: of or concerning any recent (later) *generation,* a particular stage in the development of a product, technology or the like. Page 3.

latrine: a toilet, especially one for use by a large number of people. Page 78.

lead: a heavy, bluish-gray metallic chemical element that bends easily. It is used in car batteries, pipes, solder and as a radiation shield. If lead is absorbed into the body, it can damage the nervous system, brain, liver and gastrointestinal tract. Page 56.

Leary, Timothy: (1920–1996) American psychologist and author who promoted the use of psychedelic drugs, particularly LSD. Page 12.

legacy: something highly valued that is passed on as a gift to others. Page 57.

legion: constituting a large number; many. Page 10.

leukemia: any of several cancerous disorders of blood-forming tissues, such as bone marrow, preventing normal production of red and white blood cells in the body. Leukemia results in such things as impaired blood clotting, fevers and increased susceptibility to infection. It is sometimes fatal. Page 50.

lexicon: the vocabulary of a subject, a group of people or the like. Page 14.

licit: legal; lawful. Page 2.

lid on, keep the: curb or restrain (something). Page 2.

lieu of, in: in place of; instead of. Page 82.

life-hostile: that makes life difficult. *Hostile* here means situations and conditions that make it difficult to achieve something (such as living). Page 34.

***Life* magazine:** a weekly American picture magazine published between 1936 and 1972 and focused on photojournalism. It reappeared in 1978 as a monthly magazine. Page 12.

light, bringing to: revealing or making known. Page 38.

likes of, the: such a person as; a person of the particular sort referred to. Page 30.

listening post: a city or other location viewed as a place from which information or intelligence may be obtained, from the literal sense of an advanced, concealed position near the enemy's lines, for detecting the enemy's movements by listening. Page 13.

litany: a long and often repeated list (of something, such as complaints, problems, etc.). Page 36.

lithium: a soft, very light chemical element used by psychiatry since the late 1940s as a supposed treatment for manic depression. Some of the side effects from its use are nausea, stomach cramps, diarrhea, thirstiness, blurred vision, confusion, abnormal muscle movement and pulse irregularities. Page 36.

lobotomized: subjected to a *prefrontal lobotomy,* a psychiatric operation carried out by boring holes into the skull, entering the brain and severing the nerve pathways in the two frontal lobes, resulting in the patient becoming an emotional vegetable. Page 11.

lock up: become fixed or immobile; stuck. Page 42.

lodge: become fixed, implanted or caught in a place or position; come to rest; stick. Page 4.

logical: (of an action, event, etc.) seeming natural, reasonable or sensible. Page 30.

long-range: extending into the future. Page 27.

lore: acquired knowledge or wisdom on a particular subject, for example, local traditions, handed down by word of mouth and usually in the form of stories or historical anecdotes. Page 13.

LSD: a type of hallucinogen that was originally used by psychiatrists to bring about temporary psychotic breaks in patients and became widely used illegally in the 1960s. Mild effects produced by low doses can include feelings of detachment from the surroundings, emotional swings and an altered sense of space and time. With higher doses, visual disturbances and illusions occur. Large dosages can be fatal. LSD is an abbreviation for the chemical compound *l(y)s(ergic acid) d(iethylamide).* Page 11.

Luce, Henry: Henry Robinson Luce (1898–1967), American publisher and editor. Page 12.

lysergic acid: the drug LSD, an abbreviation for the chemical name *lysergic acid diethylamide. See also* **LSD.** Page 12.

M

Mafia: a secret Italian organization allegedly engaged in smuggling, trafficking in narcotics and other criminal activities in Italy and elsewhere. Page 13.

"magic mushroom": a type of mushroom found in Mexico and the southwestern US, containing a *hallucinogen,* a substance that produces marked distortion of the senses and hallucinations. Hallucinogens are also known to lead to anti-social thoughts, disorientation and confusion and generally produce the symptoms of severe insanity. *See also* **hallucination.** Page 12.

magnitude: quantity or greatness of size, extent, etc. Page 39.

maim: wound or injure (someone) so that part of the body is permanently damaged. Page 4.

majority: the greater number or part; a number more than half of the total. Page 2.

malaise: a condition of general bodily weakness or discomfort, often marking the onset of a disease. Page 21.

Manchu: a people who originally came from Manchuria (a mountainous region of northeastern China) and set up a powerful dynasty that lasted from the seventeenth century until the beginning of the twentieth century. Page 18.

mandatory: needing to be done, followed or complied with. Page 45.

manganese: a hard, brittle, grayish-white, metallic element, used chiefly in strengthening steel. Chronic manganese exposure can damage the brain, resulting in a condition with symptoms similar to Parkinson's disease, such as slurred speech, masklike face and rigidity. Page 56.

manic: relating to *mania,* a condition characterized by such behavior as abnormal excitability, excessive activity or talkativeness, etc. Page 9.

manifestation(s): a visible demonstration or display of the existence, presence, qualities or nature of something. Page 44.

manikin: a life-size model of the human body. Manikins, automobiles, houses and other structures were used at the Nevada Test Site to show the effects of radiation and blast waves. They were placed at distances from the point where the nuclear bomb was to be exploded and were sometimes photographed from protected locations during the explosion. *See also* **blast** and **Nevada.** Page 50.

Manson, Charles: (1934–) infamous and widely sensationalized criminal of the late 1960s; he had a following who lived communally on a ranch in California, practicing free love and taking drugs. He and his followers brutally murdered seven people. Manson was finally caught, found guilty and imprisoned for life. Page 13.

marijuana: a drug made from the dried leaves and flowering tops of the hemp plant. People smoke, chew or eat marijuana. It has effects of intoxication (being affected with lessened physical and mental control) and distortions of sensory perceptions. Marijuana gained widespread use in the United States in the 1960s and 1970s, becoming the second-most-used drug after alcohol. Page 33.

marines: soldiers serving in the Marine Corps (a military service of the United States) who are trained and equipped to fight in combined land, sea and air operations. Page 50.

Marks, John D.: a former officer in the US Department of State, Marks is the author of *The Search for the "Manchurian Candidate": The CIA and Mind Control* (1979). The book draws on thousands of once-classified documents to present an overview of CIA efforts to control human behavior. The title refers to the novel (and later film) *The Manchurian Candidate* by American writer Richard Condon about American soldiers in the Korean War who are brainwashed and, on returning to the US, have no memory of their capture. But one of the soldiers has been programed to kill and is part of a Communist assassination plot against various powerful political figures. Page 11.

materialistic: of the doctrine that matter is the only reality and that everything in the world, including thought, will and feeling, can be explained only in terms of matter. Page 61.

mayhem: unrestrained destruction; infliction of violent injury upon a person or thing. Page 2.

means: an action, object or system by which a result is achieved; a way of achieving or doing something. Page 4.

measured: (of speech or writing) careful and controlled; not hurried. Page 67.

mechanism(s): the means by which an effect is produced or a purpose is accomplished. Page 34.

mental image pictures: three-dimensional color pictures with sound and smell and all other perceptions, plus the conclusions and speculations of the individual. They are mental copies of one's perceptions sometime in the past. Page 40.

mercury: a heavy, silvery-white metallic element that is liquid at room temperature; quicksilver. Ingestion of mercury (for example, by eating fish caught in polluted waters) can damage the kidneys and the central nervous system, causing tremors and poor coordination and, in severe cases, brain damage. Page 56.

merited: required or called for (something, such as a course of action or the like); deserved. Page 61.

mess with: do something wrong with; cause a problem or damage, as a result. Page 61.

methamphetamine(s): a very addictive stimulant drug that is extremely harmful to the central nervous system. It brings about loss of appetite, rapid and irregular heartbeat, increased blood pressure, irritability, anxiety, confusion, convulsions and even death. Page 13.

methylphenidate: a central nervous system stimulant. *Ritalin* is a brand name for this drug. Page 3.

mg: an abbreviation for *milligram,* a unit for measuring weight, one thousandth of a gram. Page 51.

Michigan: a state in the north central United States. Page 9.

μg/ml: symbols meaning *microgram per milliliter.* A *microgram* is a unit of mass or weight equal to one millionth (*micro* = millionth, symbol *μ*) of a gram. (A gram weighs approximately .035 ounce.) A *milliliter* is a unit of volume equal to one thousandth of a liter. (A *liter* is equal to 34 ounces.) Page 77.

microscopic print: print so small it is invisible without the use of a *microscope,* a device that uses a lens or system of lenses to produce a greatly enlarged image of an object. Such print on a label would be even smaller than what is known as *fine print* (or *small print*), the detailed part of something such as a label, document or the like that is printed in small characters, often regarded with suspicion as containing unattractive conditions that, it is hoped, will not be noticed. Page 3.

mind-altering: causing pronounced changes in mood, perceptions, behavior or thought patterns. Page 37.

mineral(s): a substance naturally occurring in the earth, used for the growth and maintenance of the body structure, maintaining the digestive juices and the fluids that are found in and around cells. Unlike vitamins, minerals are inorganic (not created by living things). Minerals play an important role in many functions of the body, such as calcium (used by the body for healthy bones and teeth), magnesium (needed for proper function of the nervous system) and sodium (regulates the amount of water in the body's cells). Page 45.

minute: extremely small, as in size, amount or degree. Page 27.

misery: great mental or emotional distress; extreme unhappiness. Also, distress or suffering caused by need or poverty. Page 3.

Mississippi: a state in the southeastern United States, on the Gulf of Mexico. Page 31.

MKULTRA: code name for a covert program of the Central Intelligence Agency. With the purpose of studying mind control, interrogation and behavior modification, MKULTRA involved the secret use of many types of drugs and other methods in an attempt to alter mental states. Page 10.

ml, µg/: symbols meaning *microgram per milliliter*. A *microgram* is a unit of mass or weight equal to one millionth (*micro* = millionth, symbol μ) of a gram. (A gram weighs approximately .035 ounce.) A *milliliter* is a unit of volume equal to one thousandth of a liter. (A *liter* is equal to 34 ounces.) Page 77.

monitor: keep track of, regulate or control thoroughly (some process or operation). Page 45.

morphine: a powerful addictive drug used in medicine to relieve severe pain. Because of its painkilling properties, it can produce a feeling of indifference to what is going on in the environment. Other side effects that accompany morphine are nausea and vomiting, as well as constipation. It is sold and used illegally and if overdosed, can cause death. Page 46.

motivation: reason for doing something. Page 49.

mowed down: killed indiscriminately or in great numbers. Page 31.

MPH: an abbreviation for *Master of Public Health*. Page 57.

MS: an abbreviation for *Master of Surgery*. Page 56.

musculoskeletal: of, relating to or involving both the muscles and the skeleton (interconnected bones) of the body. Page 76.

myriad: an indefinitely great number; innumerable. Page 28.

N

narcopolitical: relating to or involving the combination or interaction of narcotics-related and political factors. Page 76.

Narcotic and Drug Research, Inc.: a nonprofit research and educational organization that works in the field of advancing scientific knowledge in the areas of drug and alcohol abuse, treatment and recovery, HIV, AIDS, youth at risk, criminal justice and other such related areas and which later became the National Development and Research Institutes, Inc. Page 30.

nausea: a feeling in the stomach that accompanies the urge to vomit. Page 47.

Nazi: of or about the National Socialist German Workers' party, which in 1933, under Adolf Hitler, seized political control of the country, suppressing all opposition and establishing a dictatorship over all activities of the people. It promoted and enforced the belief that the German people were superior and that the Jews were inferior (and thus were to be eliminated). The party was officially abolished in 1945 at the conclusion of World War II (1939–1945). *Nazi* is from the first part of the German word for the name of the party, *Nati(onalsozialistische),* which is pronounced *nazi* in German. Page 10.

Nepal: a country in southern Asia, northeast of India, in a mountainous region. Page 82.

neurological: of or relating to matters affecting the nerves and the nervous system. Page 57.

neurotoxin: a substance that damages, destroys or impairs the functioning of nerve tissue. Page 57.

neutral: having no effect on something because it is an equal balance of two or more qualities, etc. Page 33.

Nevada: a state in the western United States. In the southeastern corner of the state, approximately 65 miles (105 kilometers) north of Las Vegas, is the *Nevada Test Site,* 1,360 square miles (3,500 square kilometers) of desert where nuclear bomb tests were conducted (1951–1992). Of the more than nine hundred such tests, approximately one hundred occurred in the atmosphere, mainly during the 1950s and early 1960s, with later testing done underground. *See also* **atmospheric nuclear weapon's test** and **blast.** Page 50.

nickel: a hard, silvery-white metallic element that is resistant to corrosion and used in alloys, batteries and in electroplating. Certain forms of nickel are toxic to the lungs when inhaled into the body as dust and can cause lung cancer. Page 56.

not for nothing: for a very good reason. Page 76.

Novocain: a brand name for an anesthetic (a drug that nullifies pain) used in medicine and dentistry. Page 44.

nuclear: relating to, using or producing energy through nuclear fission or nuclear fusion. Nuclear *fission* is the splitting of the nucleus (central part) of an atom accompanied by a significant release of energy, as used in an atomic bomb. Nuclear *fusion* is the combining of atoms accompanied by a significant release of energy, as used in a hydrogen bomb. Page 34.

nursing: trying to cure or get rid of a harmful or undesirable condition. Page 75.

nutrient(s): a substance that is needed to keep a living body alive and to help it grow. Nutrients are classified as carbohydrates, proteins, fats, vitamins, minerals and water. Page 33.

O

objective: something that one's efforts or actions are intended to attain or accomplish; purpose; goal; target. Page 49.

objective process(ing): *objective* means that can be observed. *Objective processes* are processes that apply to the physical universe. They extrovert the person's attention. A Scientology *process* is a precise set of questions asked or directions given to help a person find out things about himself or life and to improve his condition. Page 63.

obscenely: in a way that is *obscene,* offensive or shocking to morality or decency. Page 2.

oil(s): a liquid fat obtained from plant seeds, animal fats, mineral deposits and other sources that is thicker than and does not dissolve in water. Oils can dissolve or break down other oils. Therefore oil taken into the body can be used to replace bad fat within the body. Page 39.

Oklahoma: a state in the south central part of the United States. Page 72.

omnipotent: having unlimited power; all-powerful. Page 20.

operating rule: a principle that works or is being used. Page 49.

opiate: a drug used for inducing sleep and relieving pain. Page 1.

ordered: having all elements in a neat, well-organized or regular arrangement. Page 45.

Oregon: a state in the northwest United States, on the Pacific coast. Page 31.

org: an abbreviation for *organization,* by which is meant a Church of Scientology. Page 70.

organism: any living thing, such as a human body, plant, animal or bacteria. Page 33.

oriented: directed or related to or toward. Page 33.

overwhelmed: affected strongly and made to feel confused or overpowered. Page 47.

oxide of nitrogen: an *oxide* is a chemical combination of oxygen and another element. *Oxide of nitrogen* is a compound of nitrogen and oxygen—for example, *nitrogen dioxide,* a highly poisonous brown gas that is often found in smog and in the exhaust from vehicles that lack pollution-control devices. Nitrogen dioxide causes respiratory irritation and is particularly harmful to the lungs. Page 56.

oxide of sulfur: an *oxide* is a chemical combination of oxygen and another element. *Oxide of sulfur* is a compound of sulfur and oxygen—for example, *sulfur dioxide,* a colorless, poisonous gas with a sharp odor. It is released into the atmosphere by burning coal, gasoline and similar substances and can irritate the eyes and respiratory system, causing violent coughing, shortness of breath, lung edema (a watery fluid in the lung) and pneumonia. Page 56.

P

pain-drug-hypnosis (PDH): a practice used by ill-intentioned people and groups in which pain, drugs and hypnotism are administered to cause a victim to become a robot and commit crimes or act in an irrational way. Page 9.

panacea: an answer or solution for all difficulties; cure-all. Page 37.

pandemic: general; universal. Page 1.

Pandora's box: in classical mythology, a box that Zeus, king of the gods, gave to Pandora, the first woman, with strict instructions that she not open it. Pandora's curiosity soon got the better of her and she opened the box. All the evils and miseries of the world flew out to afflict Mankind. Page 9.

patently: obviously, plainly or clearly. Page 4.

PCBs: an abbreviation for *polychlorinated biphenyls. See also* **polychlorinated biphenyls.** Page 56.

perceive: notice or become aware of or identify by means of the senses. Page 46.

perception: an impression of the environment that enters through the "sense channels," such as the eyes, nose and ears. There are more than fifty perceptions used by the physical body, the best known of which are sight, hearing, touch, taste and smell. Page 12.

period(s): a particular length of time; an interval of time. Page 13.

periphery: the position or state of having only a minor involvement in something. Page 10.

permeated: spread throughout; affected in every part. Page 34.

per se: a Latin phrase meaning "by itself," used to show that one is referring to something on its own, rather than in connection with other things. Page 40.

personality: the sum total of the physical, mental, emotional and social characteristics of an individual. Page 3.

pervaded: spread throughout all parts. Page 41.

perverting: changing a system, process, etc., in a bad way so that it is not what it used to be or what it should be. Page 33.

petroleum products: products that are derived from crude oil (petroleum), such as gasoline, natural gas, diesel fuel, heating oil, plastics, paint and synthetic fibers (nylon and so forth). Page 38.

peyote: a drug made from a small cactus of the same name, native to Mexico and the southwestern United States. Peyote alters perception and can produce hallucinations (a false sense perception of somebody or something that is not really there). Page 46.

pharmaceutical: involved in or associated with the preparation, sale and use of drugs and medicines. Page 3.

pharmaceuticals: drugs obtained from a pharmacy (drugstore), as different from illegal drugs. These include drugs that are sold over the counter (without prescription) and those that are prescribed by physicians, psychologists and psychiatrists. Page 2.

pharmacopeia(s): a book containing an official list of medicinal drugs, together with articles on their preparation and use. Page 52.

phenomena: plural of *phenomenon,* an observable fact or event. Page 27.

phosphorescent tree stump: decaying wood that emits a pale glow, which comes from certain types of fungi, such as fox fire, that grow on rotting wood. The glow of the light ranges from blue to green or yellow, depending on the species of fungus. Page 70.

physiological: relating to the body and how it is observed to be functioning. From the science of *physiology,* which studies the functions and activities of living organisms and their parts, including all physical and chemical processes. Page 3.

pie chart: a type of graph in which a circle is divided into sectors that each represent a proportion of the whole. Page 2.

pilot: something done or produced as an experiment or test before being made available for wider use. Page 16.

pinup girl: a girl whose physical charms, attractive personality or other glamorous qualities make her a suitable subject of a photograph pinned up on an admirer's wall. Page 10.

pivotal: of vital or critical importance. Page 20.

placid: pleasantly calm or peaceful; serene, quiet or undisturbed. Page 78.

plated: coated with a thin film of gold, silver, etc., as for ornamental purposes. Page 38.

playing against: literally, aiming or directing at, sometimes continuously. Used figuratively. Page 48.

poison(s): any substance that, when introduced into or absorbed by a living body, destroys life or injures health. The term is commonly applied to a substance capable of destroying life by rapid action and when taken in a small quantity. Page 33.

pollutant(s): a substance that is dirty or harmful to the land, air, water, etc., making it no longer pleasant or safe to use. Page 4.

polybrominated biphenyls: also called *PBBs,* highly toxic chemical compounds used as fire retardants and in the manufacture of plastics. Page 28.

polybrominated diphenyl ethers: also called *PBDEs,* a class of chemicals used as flame retardants. PBDEs persist in the environment and accumulate in living organisms, where accumulations may result in damage to the liver, thyroid and to the nervous system. Page 56.

polychlorinated biphenyls: also called *PCBs,* highly toxic chemical compounds. Since the 1930s, PCBs have been widely used in electrical insulators, flame retardants, coolants for electrical equipment, the manufacture of plastics and many other industrial applications. New production of PCBs has been banned since the late 1970s, but contamination remains since the substance does not break down readily. PCBs are known to cause skin diseases and are suspected of causing birth defects and cancer. Page 28.

pose: present or amount to. Page 35.

Post-traumatic Stress Syndrome: a condition of persistent mental and emotional stress occurring as a result of injury or severe psychological shock. Page 57.

precedent(s): a previous instance or case that is, or may be, taken as an example or rule for subsequent cases or by which some similar act or circumstance may be supported or justified. Page 18.

precipitate: cause something, usually undesirable, to happen quickly, suddenly or unexpectedly. Page 4.

predicated: based on or upon. Page 4.

premise: a proposition that forms the basis of a conclusion. Page 29.

prescribed: (of a drug) directed to be used at set times and in specified amounts. Page 2.

present time: the time which is now and which becomes the past almost as rapidly as it is observed. It is a term loosely applied to the environment existing in now: the ground, sky, walls, objects and people of the immediate environment. In other words, the anatomy of present time is the anatomy of the room or area in which you are at the moment when you view it. Page 46.

preservative: a chemical substance used to keep foods from decaying. Page 27.

"preserver(s)": same as *preservative.* Page 39.

presiding: directing and controlling the activities of a meeting, court, etc.; being in a position of authority. Page 78.

prevalence: the state of being widespread or in general use or acceptance. Page 36.

prevalent: widespread; in general use or acceptance. Page 34.

principality: an area or region considered to operate in an independent fashion, as though not under any rule but its own. Literally, a minor semi-independent state under the rule of a prince. Page 13.

process(es): 1. a continuous action, operation or series of changes taking place in a definite manner. Page 10.

2. in Scientology, a precise set of questions asked or directions given to help a person find out things about himself or life and to improve his condition. Page 62.

processes of elimination: procedures for the removal of something. Used here in reference to the usual routes (such as the pores of the skin) by which a body gets rid of unwanted particles from within it. Page 43.

processing: the application of Dianetics or Scientology techniques (called *processes*). Processes are directly concerned with increasing the ability of the individual to survive, with increasing his sanity or ability to reason, his physical ability and his general enjoyment of life. Also called *auditing.* Page 11.

proffered: offered for consideration or acceptance. Page 41.

Prohibition: a period in the United States (1920–1933) in which the manufacture, transportation and sale of alcoholic liquors for beverage purposes were forbidden by federal law. Many people ignored the national ban. Page 18.

proliferation: a rapid (and often excessive) spread or increase of something. Page 5.

prone to: likely to or liable to suffer from, do or experience something, typically something regrettable or unwelcome. Page 14.

proofed: made resistant or not capable of being affected. Page 76.

prospects: the outlook for the future. Page 34.

proven: tested and shown to be true. Page 52.

Prozac: a drug developed by the American pharmaceutical company Eli Lilly in the late 1980s that became the largest-selling antidepressant in the world. Page 30.

psychedelia: the world of people, phenomena or items associated with *psychedelic drugs,* those drugs (such as LSD) capable of producing hallucinations and other abnormal psychic effects resembling mental illness. Page 9.

psychedelic: of or relating to the time period or culture associated with *psychedelic drugs,* those drugs (such as LSD) capable of producing hallucinations and other abnormal psychic effects resembling mental illness. Page 12.

psychopharmacological: having to do with drugs and their effects on the mind. Page 3.

psychopolitical: characterized by the interaction of politics or political events and behavior, especially in attempting to manipulate behavior and personality in order to accomplish political ends. Page 5.

psychosomatic: *psycho* refers to mind and *somatic* refers to body; the term *psychosomatic* means the mind making the body ill or illnesses which have been created physically within the body by the mind. A description of the cause and source of psychosomatic ills is contained in *Dianetics: The Modern Science of Mental Health*. Page 21.

psychotherapeutics: the nonmedical use of pharmaceutical drugs. Page 3.

psychotherapy: from psyche (soul) and therapy (to cure). A means of improving an individual's mental or spiritual condition. Page 21.

psychotropic: affecting mental activity, behavior or perception. Page 1.

purge: get rid of or remove something undesirable. Page 80.

"Purple Haze": a slang name for a type of LSD produced as a purple-colored tablet. Page 16.

pursue: try hard to achieve or obtain something, such as a goal. Page 48.

Q

quelling: suppressing; putting an end to. Page 76.

quotient: a degree or amount of a specified quality. Page 30.

R

racing: (of the heart) beating much faster than usual as, for example, out of nervousness. Page 47.

radiation sickness: a medical condition caused by overexposure to radiation as the result of therapeutic treatment, accidental exposure or an atomic bomb explosion. Symptoms include fatigue, headache, vomiting, diarrhea, loss of hair and teeth and, in severe cases, hemorrhaging (uncontrolled bleeding). Page 52.

radioactive: used to describe a substance that sends out harmful energy in the form of streams of very small particles due to the decay (breaking down) of atoms within the substance. This energy can be damaging or fatal to the health of people exposed to it. Page 34.

rancid: (of oil or of foods containing fat or oil) smelling or tasting unpleasant as a result of being stale. Page 39.

Rand Corporation: a nonprofit research organization that studies both military and nonmilitary policy problems of the United States. Though it is an independent corporation, most of the Rand

Corporation finance is from the US Department of Defense. It was begun in 1946 as *Project RAND,* standing for Research and Development. Page 13.

rational: being in full possession of (one's) reason; sane. Page 37.

ravaging: seriously destructive, damaging or ruinous. Page 41.

raw deal: harsh or unfair treatment. Page 69.

reaction(s): an instance of responding to something in a particular way or with particular behavior. Page 30.

reactivate: start working or happening again (or be made to start working or happening again) after a period of time has passed. Page 15.

recombination: the process of joining together again or differently to form substances. Page 61.

recur: happen or appear once again or repeatedly. Page 52.

regimen: 1. a regulated system, as of diet, exercise, manner of living, etc., intended to preserve or restore health or to attain some result. Page 4.

2. a specific system, program, plan or course of action to attain some result. Page 43.

reinforced: made stronger by providing additional external support. Page 48.

relapse: fall back into an undesirable state or way of life after a period of improvement. Page 42.

repercussions: effects or results, often indirect or remote, of some event or action. Page 13.

replete: abundantly supplied or provided; filled. Page 78.

reportedly: according to what some people say. Page 36.

repository: a storehouse; a source or supply of something. Page 4.

residual: present or existing, often with the sense of being a quantity left over at the end of an action. Page 4.

restimulate(d): reactivate a past memory. *See also* **restimulation.** Page 41.

restimulation: the reactivation of a past memory due to similar circumstances in the present approximating circumstances of the past. Page 48.

restimulative: causing restimulation. Page 48.

revelation: an action or instance of the showing or revealing of the truth about something. Page 1.

rhetoric: language calculated to have a persuasive or impressive effect. Page 5.

rid(ding): make someone or something free of (something unwanted). Page 16.

riddled: full of; affected with something undesirable that is spread throughout. Page 35.

Ritalin: a type of amphetamine that is the most prescribed drug in the world for the supposed psychiatric disorder of Attention Deficit Hyperactivity Disorder (ADHD). It is prescribed to adults and children and is highly addictive. *See also* **amphetamine.** Page 36.

Royal Swedish Academy of Sciences: an independent nongovernmental organization headquartered in Stockholm, Sweden. The main goal of the academy is to promote scientific research and defend the freedom of science. Page 56.

rub: an obstruction or difficulty that hinders, stops or alters the course of an argument, chain of thought or action. Page 20.

rundown: a series of steps which are processes (drills and exercises) that have specific indicators for completion and are designed to handle a specific aspect of an individual's accumulated upsets, pains, failures, etc. Page 41.

run out: exhaust the negative influence of (something); get rid of. Page 52.

S

saddle, in the: in control of something; in a position to direct or command. Page 9.

safeguard(s): something that is designed to protect from harm, risk or danger. Page 40.

sales pitch: the statements made, arguments used and assurances given by somebody trying to sell something. Page 3.

Santa Monica: a city in southwestern California, on the Pacific Ocean; a suburb of Los Angeles. Page 13.

schizophrenic(s): a person with two (or more) apparent personalities. *Schizophrenia* means scissors or *two*, plus *head*. Literally, *splitting of the mind,* hence, *split personality.* Page 46.

Scientology: Scientology is the study and handling of the spirit in relationship to itself, universes and other life. The term Scientology is taken from the Latin *scio,* which means "knowing in the fullest sense of the word," and the Greek word *logos,* meaning "study of." In itself the word means literally "knowing how to know." Page 1.

scourge: something that causes great trouble or suffering. From the literal meaning of *scourge,* a whip used as an instrument of punishment. Page 50.

sedative(s): a drug used to bring about sleepiness and temporarily relieve pain and nervousness or agitation. Page 4.

self-determinism: the condition of being *self-determined,* having power of choice and the ability to direct self or to determine the actions of self. Page 81.

set off: made (something) start happening. Page 47.

severe: causing discomfort or distress; difficult to endure. Page 46.

shooting gallery: a place where drug addicts can buy and inject themselves with narcotic drugs. Page 2.

short, in: introducing a summary statement of what has been previously stated in a few words; in summary. Page 35.

show of hands: the action of holding up the hand above the head, as a means by which the members of an assembly indicate their vote or judgment upon a proposition, a proposal, etc. Page 3.

shrugged off: dismissed or disregarded as unimportant. Page 18.

side effect(s): an undesirable secondary effect of a drug or other form of medical treatment, such as headaches, weight gain, depression, etc. Page 30.

sign of the times: something that shows what things are like now, especially things that need to be corrected. Page 16.

silica: a glassy, very hard mineral, silicon dioxide, commonly found as sand. Very fine particles of silica, known as *silica dust,* if inhaled, can lead to lung diseases and cancer. Page 56.

singularly: extraordinarily; remarkably; to an unusual degree or extent. Page 5.

Sirhan Sirhan: Sirhan Bishara Sirhan, Jordanian immigrant found guilty of the assassination of US political leader Robert F. Kennedy (1925–1968) in June 1968. Page 10.

slings and arrows: figuratively, calamity or misfortune, opposition, assault, etc. A reference to a passage from Shakespeare's tragedy *Hamlet,* in which Prince Hamlet of Denmark seeks to avenge the murder of his father. In one part of the play, Hamlet considers suicide:

> *"To be, or not to be: that is the question:*
> *Whether 'tis nobler in the mind to suffer*
> *The slings and arrows of outrageous fortune,*
> *Or to take arms against a sea of troubles,*
> *And by opposing end them?"* Page 71.

social scientist: one who studies *social science,* the study of people in society and how individuals relate to one another. Page 21.

socioeconomic: of, pertaining to or signifying the combination or interaction of social and economic factors. Page 2.

sociological: relating to social needs and problems. Also, having to do with *sociology,* the study of the individuals, groups and institutions that make up human society, including the way the members of a group respond to one another. Page 15.

sociopolitical: of, about or signifying the combination or interaction of social and political factors. Page 13.

solvent(s): a substance, especially a liquid, that can dissolve other substances. Page 38.

somatic(s): physical pains or discomforts of any kind. It can mean actual pain such as that caused by a cut or a blow. Or it can mean discomfort as from heat or cold. It can mean itching. In short, anything physically uncomfortable. Page 52.

spaced-out: inattentive, dazed, confused or lightheaded from, or as if from, drug use. Page 14.

spawned: brought forth; produced. Page 5.

speculations: conclusions or opinions reached by thinking or the consideration of some subject. Page 64.

spillover: a quantity of something spilled over; overflow; a spreading from one thing to another. Page 13.

spiritual: of or relating to or consisting of a *spirit,* the life force of an individual. Page 1.

spiritual gain: personal betterment in terms of an individual's own perceptions and abilities. Page 48.

spoiling: becoming rotten and unfit to eat because of decay. Page 39.

stampede: a sudden, headlong running away of a group of frightened animals, especially cattle or horses. Page 50.

startling: creating sudden surprise or wonder; astonishing. Page 28.

stimulant(s): anything that temporarily increases the activity of some vital process or of some organ—specifically any food, beverage or other agent that temporarily increases the activity of such a process or organ. Page 2.

stimulate: cause physical activity in something, such as a nerve or an organ. Page 35.

stringently: (of regulations or procedures) strictly controlled by rule or standard; not loose; rigidly. Page 45.

strung out: suffering from the physical or mental effects of addiction to a narcotic drug. Page 87.

study pack: also called *course pack,* a collection of reference materials to be covered by a student on a course. Page 71.

stumbling block: an obstacle or hindrance to progress or understanding. Page 4.

subjected (to): made to undergo or experience (something unpleasant). Page 10.

subjective: existing in the mind; dependent on the mind or on an individual's perception for its existence, as opposed to objective. Page 66.

substance abuse: the excessive consumption or misuse of any substance—especially drugs or alcohol—for the sake of its nontherapeutic effects on the mind or body. Page 9.

Summer of Love: the summer of 1967, a term used in reference to the gathering of young people in Haight-Ashbury for counterculture celebrations during the late spring and summer of 1967. *See also* **counterculture** and **Haight-Ashbury.** Page 16.

supplement: (said of one's diet) improve by adding one or more substances with a particular nutritional value to make up for a deficiency. Page 45.

supplement(s): a thing that is added to something else to improve or complete it, such as vitamin supplements taken in addition to what one usually eats. Page 4.

surface, on the: to outward appearances or when examined superficially. Page 3.

sweat-out: the action of releasing and eliminating impurities from the body while in a sauna or the period of time in which this is done. Page 43.

syndicate: a group of gangsters (members of a gang of criminals) who control organized crime or one type of crime, especially in one region of the country. Page 13.

syndrome: the pattern of symptoms that characterize or indicate a particular condition. Page 28.

synthesize: produce or make a chemical substance by combining simpler substances together. Page 12.

system: the entire human body, or a part of it, considered as a functioning unit. Page 15.

systemic model: *systemic* refers to something that affects or is spread throughout a whole group or system (such as an economy, market or society as a whole). A *model* is an example, representation or simplified description of something that typifies or categorizes what occurs on a widespread basis. A research project on criminal justice in New York, in categorizing different types of drug-related violence, used the phrase *systemic model* to describe the type of violence that comes about from illegal drug use. Page 30.

T

telltale: serving to reveal or disclose something that is not intended to be known. Page 3.

terminal: beyond hope, rescue or saving. Page 1.

thetan: the living unit, the individual or actual identity as distinct from the body. The word is taken from the Greek letter theta (θ), the mathematical symbol used in Scientology to indicate the source of life and life itself. Page 70.

Thorazine: a brand of *chlorpromazine,* a chemical substance used in psychiatry as a major tranquilizer. Thorazine is given to psychiatric patients who are considered violent. Page 36.

three-dimensional: having, or seeming to have, the three measurable extents (dimensions) of height, width and depth. A cube is three-dimensional and a square is two-dimensional, having only height and width. Page 46.

Tibet: a land in south central Asia, which has been part of China since the 1950s. Before China took control, Tibet was traditionally a religious kingdom, with Buddhist monks having a strong voice in its rule. Tibet's religion is a branch of Buddhism that seeks to find release from the suffering of life and attain a state of complete happiness and peace. Page 69.

tidal wave: any widespread or powerful movement or tendency. Literally, a *tidal wave* is a large, destructive ocean wave, especially one caused by an underwater earthquake or volcanic eruption. Page 14.

time track: the consecutive record of mental image pictures which accumulates through a person's life. Page 46.

tissue(s): organic body material in humans, animals and plants made up of large numbers of cells that are similar in form and function. The four basic types of tissue are nerve, muscle, skin and connective (which support and hold parts of the body together). Page 4.

top dog: the most important or powerful person; a person that has acquired a position of highest authority. Page 9.

toxicology: the branch of science concerned with the nature, effects and detection of poisons and their antidotes. Page 56.

toxin(s): originally, a poison produced by a living organism, which is capable of causing disease. The word later came to refer to any substance said to accumulate in the body, which is considered harmful or poisonous to the system. Page 1.

"tracking": following and understanding what is going on around one. Page 63.

tranquilizer(s): any of certain drugs given as a supposed calming agent in controlling various emotional conditions. Page 33.

transgressions: acts or instances of violating or breaking mores, laws or moral codes. Page 76.

trauma: emotional shock following a stressful event. Page 65.

travail: pain or suffering resulting from conditions that are mentally or physically difficult to overcome. Page 61.

trigger: bring about or cause to occur. Page 27.

"trip(s)": an experience undergone by someone taking drugs such as LSD or any similar drug. A "trip" can involve a range of sensations from mild to intense and often consists of euphoria (a false feeling of elation) and hallucination (the perception of objects with no reality and the experiencing of sensations without any external cause). These experiences can also occur to someone who took drugs in the past, even without taking them in the present. Page 12.

turn on: cause to start operating or appear, as if by means of a switch, button or valve; activate. Page 51.

U

UCLA: an abbreviation for *University of California at Los Angeles,* one of the several campuses, located in various parts of the state, that form the *University of California,* a state-supported educational institution founded in the 1800s. The UCLA campus offers degrees in arts and sciences, humanities, business, architecture, engineering, law and the health professions. Page 56.

ultimate: 1. most extreme. Page 37.

2. lying beyond all others; forming the final aim or object. Page 49.

ultimately: basically and fundamentally. Page 4.

umbrella: something, such as an organization or policy, that covers or includes a number of groups or elements. Page 10.

underpinning: that which forms the basis or foundation of something. Literally, a system of supports beneath a wall or the like. Page 20.

unequivocal: conclusive and absolute, not subject to conditions or exceptions. Page 28.

unique: being the only one of its kind. Page 20.

unleash: set something free, as if from a leash or other form of restraint or confinement. Page 47.

unmitigated: absolute, outright. Page 13.

unrelenting: not easing or lessening in strength, speed or effort. Page 37.

upper atmosphere: the part of the atmosphere (mixture of gases surrounding the Earth) lying higher than the most immediate layer, that is, the atmosphere beyond 10 miles (16 kilometers) above the surface of the Earth. Page 40.

Utah: a state in the western United States. Page 78.

V

Valium: an addictive tranquilizing drug often prescribed by doctors or psychiatrists to "relieve" anxiety or tension. Page 36.

vantage point: a position or location that provides a broad view or perspective of something. Page 14.

vast: very great in extent or degree. Page 33.

vein: manner or direction of thought. Page 63.

veritable: being true or real; not false or imaginary. Page 15.

Viet Cong: a member or supporter of the Communist-led armed forces of the National Liberation Front of South Vietnam that fought to unite the country with North Vietnam between 1954 and 1976. *See also* **Vietnamese.** Page 13.

Vietnamese: of *Vietnam,* a tropical country in Southeast Asia, site of a major war from 1954 to 1975 between South Vietnam and Communist-controlled North Vietnam. The United States became involved in the mid-1960s, lending its support to South Vietnam. By the late 1960s, due to the length of the war, high US casualties and US participation in war crimes against the Vietnamese, American involvement became increasingly unpopular in the US and was strongly protested. In 1973, despite continuing hostilities between North and South Vietnam, the US removed all its troops. By 1975, the Communists had overrun South Vietnam and the war was officially ended, leading to the unification of the country (1976) as the Socialist Republic of Vietnam. Page 13.

vigor: energy, force or enthusiasm. Page 44.

Virginia: a state in the eastern United States, south of Washington, DC. Page 9.

vis-à-vis: in relation to. Page 76.

vitality: great energy and liveliness; a large amount of physical and mental energy, usually combined with a wholehearted and joyous approach to situations and activities. Page 29.

vitamin B$_1$: a vitamin found in green peas, beans, egg yolks, liver and the outer coating of cereal grains. It assists in the absorption of carbohydrates and enables carbohydrates to release the energy required for cellular function. A *carbohydrate* is one of the three main classes of food (the others are fats and protein) that provide energy to the body. Page 37.

volitional: of or related to the act of consciously choosing. Page 64.

volume: a large quantity or amount of something. Page 34.

vying: competing strongly in order to obtain or achieve something. Page 34.

W

warden(s): the chief (highest) administrative officer in charge of a prison. Page 70.

washout curve: the graphic representation of the change occurring over a period of time (curve) concerning the elimination of drugs or chemicals from the body (washout). Page 77.

waste(s): 1. a failure to use something wisely, properly, fully or to good effect. Page 20. 2. an unwanted or unusable byproduct of something, such as radiation. Page 34.

what cost the suffering?: a rhetorical question (one that is asked for effect rather than to get information) implying that there is no way to measure what the loss is to those who have experienced pain and suffering. Page 2.

wheat rust: a fungus that attacks the roots of wheat plants and produces reddish marks on the stems and leaves. Page 42.

World Health Organization: an agency of the United Nations established in 1948 with the stated purpose of improving the health of the world's people and preventing or controlling communicable diseases. Page 56.

World Trade Center (WTC): a complex in New York City that included twin skyscrapers (the tallest in the US at 110 stories). These buildings were destroyed on September 11 (9/11), 2001, when two jetliners, hijacked by terrorists, were flown into them, causing the worst building disaster in recorded history and the deaths of some 2,800 people. Page 28.

wreak: bring about (harm, damage, etc.); cause, inflict. Page 27.

wrought: brought about or caused. Page 87.

X

X-rays: invisible waves consisting of tiny particles of energy that are able to go through soft materials in the same way light passes through glass. When this occurs, energy is transferred to the material and damage can result. They are called *X-rays* as, at the time of their discovery, they were rays of unknown origin. They are commonly used by hospitals and doctors to show pictures of the inside of the body. Page 40.

Z

zoned-out: lost awareness of one's immediate surroundings or one's cares or troubles, through the means of daydreaming or taking drugs. Page 14.

Zyprexa: a brand name for a psychiatric drug. Page 3.

INDEX

Alpert, Richard

LSD high priest, CIA-sponsored "acid" testing of, 12

Ambulance Industry Journal

L. Ron Hubbard Detoxification Program, effectiveness of, 56

"amnesia beams"

mind-control programs and, 11

amphetamines

consumption of, 1

antidepressants

consumption of, 2

anti-nerve gas

biological-warfare agents, 28

Apollo

research vessel, 14

arsenic, 35

Artichoke

code name, federal mind-control program, 10

artificial sweeteners, 39

asbestos products

workers in factories that produce or use, 38

assists, 75

atmosphere

deterioration of upper, 40

atomic power, 40

axiomatic truths

of Dianetics and Scientology, 20

B

bathing suit

niacin flush and, 51

Benitez, William

Narconon program and, 75

"Better Living through Chemistry"

multibillion-dollar sales pitch, 3

biochemical

definition, 33

biophysical handlings, 49

life-hostile elements and, 49

Black Death

drug crisis rivaling cultural waste of, 20

blankness

drugs and, 48

Bluebird

code name, federal mind-control program, 10

body

composed of, 33

disarranging of biochemistry and fluid balance of, 44

Bowart, Walter

Operation Mind Control, 11

boy soldiers, African/Asian

psychotropic drugs and, 4

brain

marijuana and atrophy of, 36

Brave New World

of drug consumption, 20

BZ

devastating effects of, 13

C

caffeine

drug, 35

cancer, 39

canned soup, 34

canned vegetables, 34

psychiatry and, 18, 46

relapses and, 42

remaining in body, 27, 42, 44

schizophrenics and, 46

sweating out deposits, 43

wheat rust, 42

Luce, Henry

CIA psychedelicizing of, 12

M

"magic mushroom"

Timothy Leary and, 12

Manchu

opium and China's last dynasty, 18

Manson, Charles

mass murderer, 13

marijuana, 33, 36

brain atrophy and, 36

mental aspects, 46

remaining in body for years, 38, 44

Marks, John D.

The Search for the "Manchurian Candidate," 11

medicine

Assistant Clinical Professor of Medicine, UCLA and effectiveness of Hubbard Detoxification Program, 56

Drug Rundown, 67

environmental medicine, 4

mental alertness

drugs and breakdown of, 36

mental aspects, 46

mental image pictures

definition, 46

drugs and, 46, 47

mentally ill

drugs and quieting, 37

mental technology

Man and adequate, 69

metals, plated

workers in factories that produce, 38

methamphetamine, 13

methylphenidates

school-age children and, 3

teenage student violence and, 3

military

Agent Orange and, 28

mind

drugs and, 70

what it is, 46

mind control

Candy Jones, World War II pinup girl and, 10

disclosed in *Science of Survival*, 11

Dorothy "Dot" Jones and, 9

testing of psychotropic compounds on US citizens, 10

MKULTRA

umbrella code name, federal mind-control program, 10

mood-altering drugs

populations conditioned to, 3

morphine

mental aspects, 46

mothers

children of drug-taking, 36

N

Narconon, 75–83

before and after statistics, 83

courses, description of, 80–81

drug-free withdrawal, 80

effectiveness of, 79

founding of, 75

LRH technologies for withdrawal and
rehabilitation employed by, 75

Narconon Arrowhead

photographs, 72–74, 78–79

training center at Lake Eufaula,
Oklahoma, 77

Narconon Nepal

drug prevention through education, 82

**Narconon New Life Detoxification
Program,** 75

**Narcotic and Drug Research Inc., New
York,** 30

nerves

alcohol and, 37

drugs and damage to, 36

New York City

Purification Program, commemorative
fireman's helmet and, 57

**New York Rescue Workers Detoxification
Project,** 28

Senior Medical Adviser on effectiveness
of L. Ron Hubbard Detoxification
Program, 57

niacin

allergies, running out, 52

"educated" vitamin, 51–55

flushes, description, 52

interacting with niacin deficiencies, 52

manifestations occurring from, 51

radiation and, 51

reactions turned on will turn off and, 52

release of toxic substances,
illustration, 47

running through past deficiencies, 52

somatics and, 52

sunburn and, 51

vitamin and mineral dosages
and, 54

vitamin B complex and, 51

Novocain

can be reactivated years after, 44

nutrition

Purification Program and, 46

O

objective processing, 63

oil

rancid, 39

Operation Mind Control

Walter Bowart's, 11

opiates

consumption of, 1

P

pain

deadening with drugs, 37

drugs and, 21, 66

pain-drug-hypnosis (PDH)

mind control, 9

painkillers, 33, 34, 37

remaining in body for years, 38

paints

workers in factories that produce or
use, 38

PBBs (polybrominated biphenyls)

study of Michigan residents exposed
to, 28

perceptions

drugs and distorted, 46

THE
L. RON HUBBARD
SERIES

"To really know life," L. Ron Hubbard wrote, "you've got to be part of life. You must get down and look, you must get into the nooks and crannies of existence. You have to rub elbows with all kinds and types of men before you can finally establish what he is."

Through his long and extraordinary journey to the founding of Dianetics and Scientology, Ron did just that. From his adventurous youth in a rough and tumble American West to his far-flung trek across a still mysterious Asia; from his two-decade search for the very essence of life to the triumph of Dianetics and Scientology—such are the stories recounted in the L. Ron Hubbard Biographical Publications.

Drawn from his own archival collection, this is Ron's life as he himself saw it. With each volume of the series focusing upon a separate field of endeavor, here are the compelling facts, figures, anecdotes and photographs from a life like no other.

Indeed, here is the life of a man who lived at least twenty lives in the space of one.

FOR FURTHER INFORMATION VISIT
www.lronhubbard.org

To order copies of *The L. Ron Hubbard Series*
or L. Ron Hubbard's Dianetics and
Scientology books and lectures, contact:

US AND INTERNATIONAL

BRIDGE PUBLICATIONS, INC.
5600 E. Olympic Blvd.
Commerce, California 90022 USA
www.bridgepub.com
Tel: (323) 888-6200
Toll-free: 1-800-722-1733

UNITED KINGDOM AND EUROPE

NEW ERA PUBLICATIONS
INTERNATIONAL ApS
Smedeland 20
2600 Glostrup, Denmark
www.newerapublications.com
Tel: (45) 33 73 66 66
Toll-free: 00-800-808-8-8008